Aging Is a Full Time Job

Now is the time to
make peace with your past
so you don't mess up the present!

By

Marcia Casar Friedman

Copyright © 2010 Marcia Casar Friedman

ISBN: 978-1-60910-554-9

Library of Congress Control Number: 2010914656

Printed in the United States of America.

BookLocker.com, Inc.
2010

Disclaimer

The self-help contents are solely the opinion of the author and should not be considered as a form of therapy, advice, direction, and/or diagnosis or treatment of any kind, whether medical, spiritual, mental, or other. The author shall not be liable for any loss incurred as a consequence of the use and application, directly or indirectly, of any information presented in this work.

If expert advice or counseling is appropriate, seek the services of a competent professional. The self-help resources in this book are not intended to be a substitute for therapy.

The purchaser or reader of this publication assumes responsibility for the use of these materials and information.

Special Thank You To:

Manny and Helen Casar, my parents

Uncle Carl Jack Unger, my favorite character

Aunt Edith Casar, who honored Mom's request to
take care of me as if I were her own daughter

With major appreciation to my son, Hal Edward Friedman,
for choosing me as his Mom

Author Biography

Marcia Casar Friedman is an author from California. She was a teacher for the Pittsburgh Public Schools, the Los Angeles School District, and a Master Training Teacher for Cal State Northridge.

Writing, psychology, and sociology have always been her passions. Marcia conducted adult training programs in English as a second language, created and led "feelings workshops," behavior modification classes and was a trainer in various industries.

Retirement gave Marcia the opportunity to follow her passion to use life experiences to write books for the 50+ age group, with an emphasis on Silver Sages.

Aging Is a Full Time Job

Contents

Introduction

Dear Reader:

Let's talk!

Thank you for going on a journey of self-awareness with me. I hope you learn more about the unique person you are aging into, as a one of a kind silver sage.

To work with the ups and downs in life, we need to consciously create a steadiness. Make ongoing changes and adjustments to maintain a sense of balance in order to become a happier, more successful person.

How many resumes have you written in your lifetime? Too many?

They focus attention on your background of work experiences, especially transferable skills. My initial plan was to write a life script or memoir, to review my life to this point, as my personal review or resume for this phase of my job, called aging. I was motivated to better understand and improve my present, as well as my future, as a silver sage.

I realized it was important for me to share the tools I have learned for others to discover their own path, and be encouraged to pass the torch.

Included in each chapter, are many personal and private life experiences. This book is definitely nonfiction!

My natural style is to have a conversation to explain, analyze and teach, whether I'm in or out of the classroom. I'm not the kind of person who learns something, then keeps it to herself. I want everyone to learn too!

I've analyzed my life stories to discover how I think those events would be different today. A magical crystal ball would be required to figure it out. How often I've asked myself, if I knew then, what I know now, how different would my life be today? Decisions can only be made by using the tools available at the time.

I encourage you to broaden your scope by reading my stories and writing your own life story. Love yourself even though you aren't perfect! If I have not helped you to accomplish any of these goals, then move on to more challenging opportunities.

Writing is healing, no matter how you do it. Three basic approaches exist for the mechanics of writing: (1) put pen or pencil to paper, (2) type on a computer or typewriter, (3) talk into a recorder, or talk with another person, if you cannot physically write.

The understandings I've gained, come from several sources, such as my experiences of living long enough to become a silver sage. Also observing and hearing incidents from others while absorbing all of the available information from every event attended. Add a lifetime of research and problem solving to the mix.

For most of my mid-adult life, I was known as "Mama Marcia" because peers and family came to me for advice. Writing has given me the opportunity to spread my wings.

I urge you to seek professional help if life becomes overwhelming. Feeling overpowered happens to all of us at one time or another. Counseling can be tremendously helpful. I am not a professional medical or psychological therapist.

> **Don't ask yourself what the world needs.**
> **Ask yourself what makes you come alive**
> **and then go and do that.**
> **Because what the world needs, is people**
> **who have come alive.**
> **–Harold Whitman**

Part One: *Aging*

1

Who Are the Silver Sages?

The idea of calling my generation the "silver sages" comes from our graying hair and our enlightened wisdom. No matter what you know or how much you have learned, more insight is gained from living life every day.

Praise and encourage yourself now! It has taken you many years of great effort to become more competent in your work and more skillful in your relationships. Also, more knowledgeable about the interactions between your family members and more adept at accepting the surprises life presents to you. About the only thing that comes without effort is natural aging.

Being referred to as a "silver sage" is much more acceptable than being called elderly or old. Silver sages learn many guiding words of wisdom and hopefully, freely give them to others. At Elder Wisdom Circle, a free website, anyone can ask a question and receive an answer within a few days. They are also looking for online senior volunteers. Interested? Visit: www.elderwisdomcircle.org

The sixty-somethings all have one stage of life in common. I call this phase of development, the senior crisis.

It takes many years of hard work to get over the commotion of the midlife crises in order to find a more productive path to a happier life.

Then, little by little, the things we worked so hard for don't haunt us anymore. Don't get too comfortable. It's time to move on! A silver sage is on a journey full of learning possibilities plus many changes. The time has come to share instinctive wisdom. I do savor being a work in progress!

In my mid-sixties, I recognized how much the evolution of the career senior crisis was disrupting my life. The old routine of competing with younger job seekers had to end. It was time to give up the horrid chase for a better work life, hoping it would lead to a position in top management along, with the alleged promise of a big bucks salary with bonuses. How exhausting! Every day, age discrimination continues to be alive and well. I wanted to be the real me, not the pretend me.

Ongoing advances in the field of medicine have made it possible to live longer than ever before. While a longer life provides opportunities for those sixty-five and older to do things that had been put on hold to raise families and work, it can also create a feeling of isolation and loneliness. The new concept of working an encore career has great merit for anyone who wants to retire from the drudgery of a job and find a new career. www.encore.org is a helpful web site for seniors wanting to research career changes.

Women are known to be the family shoppers. For this reason, companies gear their goods to women's buying preferences. Products for women are more expensive than are those for men.

Manufacturers add some perfume to beauty products, hike up the price, and advertise them for women. Men's shirts are wrinkle free and easy care. Occasionally, a women's blouse is wrinkle resistant, with a stiffness or polyester added. Why can't the fabric content be the same for women's clothes as it is for men, to keep the price down and stop the insanity of ironing? These ideas are not just for seniors, but also for people of all ages.

We need more monthly magazines geared to the interests and changes experienced by seniors. Which silver sage does not know tricks to spending less money in the grocery store? These aren't new ideas to us. We've been clipping coupons for as long as coupons have existed. The senior crisis repeatedly showed me how I'm in a different stage of life than I was during all those years when I devoured those helpful family magazines and wanted those useful products. It's time for us to move on to new interests and to receive new advice. Where are the broad spectrum magazines for senior lifestyles?

Are you ready to start a new helpful career in magazine publications? Ask senior authors to share their writings.

Yes, the senior crisis moves us forward to get prepared for the time when we don't even want to think about running a marathon or eating a whole cheese cake that will activate lactose intolerance and colitis, and, and, and . . .

What? You didn't hear my question? If not hearing or understanding conversations happens to you, there can be several causes. It could be selective hearing, in order to not have to pay attention, because we don't care about the conversation. Seniors can and do ask for a repeat. If speakers show irritation or a lack of patience, that is their problem, not ours.

Sometimes, a hearing problem is caused by trying to pay attention to more than one thing at a time. This happens on the phone and in personal conversations. In these situations, it is important to slow down to tune into one conversation to understand what is said. Be a silver sage with the wisdom to solve problems. Clearly analyze the problem, write down every possible solution, then decide on the solution that seems like it will provide the best outcome.

Most of today's problem solving techniques came from past learning experiences. My first car was a used, deep maroon two-door 1954 Pontiac. Oh, how exciting it was to drive my very own car. It was a tasteful car, highly recommended by the dealer. The first day I owned it; I drove right from the dealer to a shopping area, parked the car, put a dime in the parking meter, and went in the drugstore for shampoo. Such freedom, pride in car ownership, maturity, and joy to have my own car!

Within fifteen minutes, I was back from the store, sitting in the car, anxious to drive around town. It would not start! No matter what I did, it would make a grinding noise or it would stay silent, but the engine would not turn over.

I found a payphone, called my dad, and sobbed while describing the frustrations over my new car. Mr. Fix-it Dad was not a car person, but he would do anything he could to help solve my problems. The dealer told him to let the car sit, and wait for it to cool off. Not wanting to feed the parking meter any more money, I waited and waited, walking around the area near the car. Getting in and out of the car several times only made me more impatient. Three hours later, the car started!

The wise advice from the car salesman solved the problem, but at what an emotional cost! The problem kept occurring the next couple of days, leaving me stranded several times to wait for the car to cool down.

The anguish wasn't worth having the car. As a result, I paid more money to buy a newer used car, but only after Dad asked every question he could think of and hired a mechanic to inspect the engine.

Aging enables us to build on problem solving skills from the past. Keep asking questions! We will never be familiar with everything there is to know. Of this, I am sure; every problem has at least two solutions.

Car prices are outrageous today, even though they have become disposable early in their lifespan. How can it be possible to put a man on the moon, send a fax to a foreign country, retrieve information from a computer, and watch a war on TV, but we can't find an alternative fuel patterned after a battery to keep a car running for at least three years? Since car doors often get dings when in parking spaces, why doesn't someone invent a set of safety strips to cushion the side of the car, thus preventing the dings? And my favorite question--Why can't we have tires that never go flat and don't wear out before the car wears out?

That's me, asking my typical "why" questions. Silver sages don't just accept answers and ideas. We ask thought provoking questions, especially when the answer given to us doesn't sound right. We must learn to trust our own instincts gained from years of a variety of experiences.

Today, sales people continue the practices of pushing the product to the uninformed and to unsuspecting seniors. Buyers beware, be very aware! It's important to ask for help, especially when treading in unknown territory. I'm not interested in the promissory sales pitch games anymore, from anyone in any industry. Patience is supposed to come with aging? Not when the situation is obviously illogical or noticeably incorrect. My inner gut knows the truth. Preying on unsuspecting, naïve seniors of any age is unacceptable!

I don't know much more about buying a car today, then I did when I bought my first car. Dad taught me to ask questions and get help. The same advice applies today, especially with all the new technology available.

It's never too late to reinvent yourself. Being a silver sage led me to realize how important it is to make positive changes that would affect the rest of my life. Aging is a journey of change.

A key idea is to strive to keep the timeless treasurers from life and let go of the useless details. Create a balance to unclutter the things and people in your life. Seniors no longer smugly say they can predict what they will or will not do in given situations.

We know the frustrations of prejudging, only to find ourselves wrong. Listen, learn, and then decide each individual situation by using the insights from the past. Change is necessary and possible, with a lot of awareness and work.

The standards once used to measure success don't apply to modern silver sages. It's time to see aging in a new way and to value the new model.

Been there, done that! Give up the standards previously used to measure success like being busy all the time, fueling the goals of climbing the corporate ladder or increased earnings to purchase more material things. The unique capacity of seniors to see the methods by which the past, present, and future interact, provides the foundation for sharing wisdom with the young.

The old obsolete view was to accept all seniors as descending downhill with a deficiency in mental, emotional, and physical capacities. Who said you can't teach an old dog new tricks? Give me a break! Comparing seniors to old dogs is an outrageous tag. It's a new world!

The wisdom of silver sages is remarkable, despite the fact that everyone has been spiritually wounded in the past. Those experiences pave the way to share healing wisdom learned from understanding personal stresses. Seniors are wise guides and wounded healers who have so much to give, by teaching others how to live with dignity as well as compassion.

Not enough emphasis is put on the remarkable storehouse of experiences silver sages have available to share. Instead, the negative aging processes are accentuated. Yes, the body does break down from all the stresses it has endured. Of course, it's of the utmost importance to acknowledge and care for the dis-eases (without comfort).

The new struggles involve living with the loss of good quality health, the death of a spouse, the imminence of death, or being abandoned by children who think they have better things to do than visit with dad in the nursing home. Physical and psychological resources decline, making it necessary to focus on individual differences and what people value the most.

What do you say when someone asks your age? In the work a day business world, we would not dare to sabotage our jobs by revealing gray hair or our true age. What a relief to be able to tell the truth and be proud of the chronological number. Bob Hope lived to be 100 and claimed himself to be "many ages." Seniors are a composite of all the previous years, plus this new stage of being a silver sage. Be proud, be your own hero!

Everything learned from the past stages of development continue forward into the final stage. Some things can and should be discarded, for change is the essence of life.

There are several important traits to carry on:
* Social connectedness – relationships and friendships.
* Personal growth to gain knowledge.
* Share wisdom by helping others.
* Trust yourself .
* Be self-sufficient and independent as long as possible.
* Share love, acceptance, and forgiveness.
* Laugh often.
* Simplify. Organize your daily life to live smarter with less stress.

If you truly desire to live an authentic life, embrace the spiritual journey that comes with the truth of knowing who you really are today, right now.

Create a Wish List. The best wish list is reasonable, current, and feasible. Start with creative ideas that can lead to a personal wish come true.

Write five realistic wishes with the goal of fulfilling them today or tomorrow at the latest. These straightforward desires are readily available to be granted. It is possible to make these wishes come true immediately.

1. I wish I could compliment myself. I will give two compliments to myself every day.

2. _____

3. _____

4. _____

5. _____

6. _____

7. I wish I could wear my best outfit today. I will wear my fanciest outfit during dinner.

If you have more wishes for today, keep writing. to make them come true. Tomorrow and every day, create another satisfying wish list. The encouraging results will be worthwhile.

The middle category of wishes would be the dreams you think could possibly come true. They are possible, but not always probable. It's good to create the path to push a little harder and further to have goals fulfilled.

Write five wishes that you could make come true within a month. Write them in your private journal and keep them handy to review the wishes daily. Start writing with "I will........." Such as, "I will join and attend a weekly book reading club."

More wishes might be about exercising 30 minutes per day, talking with a stranger about your wishes, buying something frivolous, taking a much desired vacation, calling an old friend to say "I'm sorry.", learning a new craft, take meditation classes, and more.

The third category of wishes represents the biggest challenges to accomplish. Some difficult personal goals are important to have too. They could take longer than a month to achieve.

Write five difficult, but maybe not all together impossible wishes. Detail them in your writing journal. Some wishes are old unfulfilled dreams and others are new ideas with new possibilities. Start with "I will..........."

This category might include eating dinner at the most expensive local restaurant, volunteer to be a standup comedian, write daily to create a book, dance with a new partner, plant a tree, travel to a foreign country, swim in an ocean, learn yoga, ride a motorcycle, paint a picture, sing in a choir, and more.

Wishes have a way of changing with aging. Updating current dreams is an ongoing process. A completely unexpected outcome can sometimes happen when the dream comes true. Every now and then, the wishing was better than the fulfillment of the dream. Some people will say planning the vacation was exciting, but the trip was boring!

A popular expression has become admired in our daily lives. What do you wish to accomplish before you die, before you kick the bucket?

A common theory declares the idiom came from the middle ages when a noose was tied around someone's neck while he or she was standing on an overturned bucket. When the pail was kicked away, the victim was hanged. They kicked the bucket and died!

A bucket list could easily dip into all three categories of wishes. The bucket list could hold easy to achieve wishes, difficult to accomplish wishes and those that are almost impossible. "Almost" is the key word here. Maybe those wishes aren't as unattainable as they seem on the surface.

What is written in your bucket list? No list? Write one in your journal.

"Before I kick the bucket, I want to………

Recognize the truth that you are much more then you imagine yourself to be.

2

Aging Does Not Make Us Forgetful

***Having way too many stupid things
to remember makes us forgetful!***

The harder I strain to try to remember, the more I forget what I'm trying to remember. When computers first came out, we were told if we put junk in, junk will come out. What a great comparison to our memory storage capacity. I'm at the corner now, but I've forgotten whether my dreams are a turn to the left or to the right. Good, let's make new dreams! Instead of storing and chasing old dreams, it's time to find and make fresh dreams.

Retirement means the end of a journey, a time to withdraw, pull back, and discovering a new interest in being your own boss. Unfortunately, retiring does not mean the bill paying will stop, nor will the fix-it projects, the personal interactions, or learning how to work the medical systems. The technological world is a lot more complicated every day, giving us more and more to learn.

Retirement means being free to follow through on these problem-solving projects without the stresses of work taking priority. There is so much less to store in my available memory without having to remember so many stupid things from the past. I acknowledge they were not stupid at the time, but now they are irrelevant.

The first joyous change of not working was adjusting to the relief of not having to remember to set the clock radio to wake me up to get ready for work. I sleep much more peacefully with the comfort of knowing I will wake up when my body is ready, and not when a jarring radio goes off.

Having time to listen calmly to the gardeners working in my townhouse complex is remarkable. They have a daily routine of sweeping, clipping, mowing, leaf blowing, and cleaning up. It's a noisy, dirty job, but they always smile politely when I go to get the newspaper at my front door.

Being relaxed in a calm daily environment enables me to remember more. How nice to release the old tensions of the job atmosphere, where employees were expected to be perfect. How nice to refresh my spirit and feel really relaxed.

Time pressures have eased. I can stay as long as I want in the bathroom. The clock on the bathroom wall still tells me the time of day. It's no longer a trigger to push me to rush around, or a generator of aggravation. The bathroom is a great quiet place to read and meditate. No additional hurrying, no more planning for the details of a busy day at work while absorbing the pressure and worry about forgetting to do something. I remember so much more now!

Meals are particularly convenient at home. I have a handy refrigerator, microwave, and all the silverware I could want. Making breakfast is a leisurely accomplishment, done on my own schedule, while reading the morning newspaper in private. Work used to dictate my lunch schedule, which included eating in uncomfortable surroundings, sometimes at my desk or in the mailroom, seated on a folding chair.

Unlike the work office, my house has flowing hot water available for me to wash my hands. Lunchtime is no longer a convoluted, annoying project with people walking in and out of the room commenting on the smells while asking questions to interrupt what could have been a quiet lunch. Who knew life could be more successful when it is balanced? Many people, but not me.

Clothing is not a big deal anymore. I don't dress to keep up with co-workers or to please bosses or clients. Freedom! I don't even have to remember which color I wore each day to avoid duplications. Spending less on clothes as well as on grooming products is a blessing.

Following store sales and keeping up with fashions are still interesting leisure time activities, but I don't feel pressured to get to a sale before everything is gone. If I see a sale advertised in the paper and forget to go in time, it doesn't create stress.

I know, I know. I have not emphasized the flawed downside of no longer working full time. Being prepared for retirement, especially with a planned, sensible financial backup would make it a lot more comfortable. Life is what you make of it! Letting go is difficult, but it must be done before moving forward. The journey to change gives us many opportunities to transform our thinking and our lives.

An idle mind is a house of worry. I love these handed down words of insight. Keep those challenges coming, instead of wasting away in front of the TV or spending days sharing illnesses with any gray haired person who will listen. In moderation, seniors pay attention to each other's complaints and are supportive. That's a good thing!

There is so much to learn with so little time. I'm learning about myself on a daily basis, tuning into myself by meditating, thinking, remembering, writing, and planning for the immediate future. There is so much to learn in general, by surfing the Internet, reading the newspaper, watching TV, and observing people living their lives. Learning never ends. I don't have to remember everything I learn. No one is pushing me to memorize facts for an upcoming test. A variety of interesting learning experiences each day is important, while I can still appreciate them.

Sometimes, I can't focus and fully concentrate because too many things are swirling around in my mind. What a straight direct line to forgetting! Worry is such a waste of energy. Calm down, breathe, and pay full attention to one thing at a time. This is what I do when I don't hear everything being said. At least I strive to do as much of the calm down routine as possible. It's not so easy for this natural born worrywart! I choose to believe senility is a gift from God so we won't be alert and aware of the role reversal when our children become our bosses!

Recently, I described to a doctor how my mind felt like an overloaded washing machine that was throwing out extra clothes. The more I keep stuffing in new information, the more my brain goes on overload to get ready to throw out new details. The results are the often discussed "senior moments" or memory lapses.

Sometimes it gets harder to remember details from the past. I'd remind myself of something then mentally work on recalling it fully. To remember, I learned to stop stressing by paying attention to other subjects. Within a short time, the recall of the past will kick in. I forget about it, to remember it!

The doctor agreed with me saying, aging and stress do cause various degrees of overload. He explained how relaxation clears the memory enough to allow the recall to return. The process works as a helpful way to keep the memory alive and active..... if the subject is important enough to remember!

Aging is not for the weak.
Stay focused and strong!

I threw out the memory of learning how to conjugate verbs and diagram sentences. When did I ever use those memorized skills in my adult life, and why do I want to remember them now? Throw out the obsolete details to make room for today's internet technology, like emailing, as well as blogging.

Forgetting people from the past, along with not remembering important rules with regulations from previous jobs are also throwaways. Over fifteen years ago, I learned several sets of public utility commission rules that governed California truckers. For me, as an auditor of truckers' insurance, it was important to know the rules as mandated by the state lawmakers. Why would I want to remember those rules now? Forget about it!

Most of us store information that was important at the time but later don't remember to get rid of the unused and unneeded, like old memorabilia from parties and vacations. Silver sages constantly learn to distinguish between the useless thoughts taking up too much memory space and remembrances that are important to keep. If we continue to recall as well as to concentrate on the old stuff, then we won't have room to remember new things.

The garage sale motto is "If you haven't used it in five years, get rid of it." Recall is needed much longer, so we must be more selective about what we discard in order to free up more memory space. What a shame we can't buy more memory for ourselves, like we can for our computers!

Forgetting names is a different matter. Though it's a great cause for concern among many seniors, it is normal. It happens! I thought I took after Dad, who forgot names when he was in his fifties. AAMI, or age-associated memory impairment is the normal forgetfulness that occurs with aging. Without other symptoms, such as from an illness, medications, or injuries from an accident, it is a common complaint. Anxiety, tiredness, lack of concentration, grieving, and perhaps no longer being interested in the person, can be the culprits. Recognize and appreciate that we have been able to remember an amazing amount of details during our lifetimes while experiencing so many stresses. If forgetting names is our worst problem, we will be fine!

I started my teaching career with two kindergarten classes a day. The real total of 75 to 90 students assigned to me daily was considered to be high average. When I estimate the number of students I taught during my career, there were definitely over a thousand names for me to remember. After all these years, most of the names are gone with the wind! Some students made such an impression on me that I naturally keep their names in my memory.

Surprisingly enough, the names coupled with physical appearances I remember most are of the children who put smiles on my face, not the time consuming troublemakers. A couple of years ago I saw my favorite former kindergarten student. He was a bank Vice President who helped me to refinance my home. To reunite with my favorite student was one of the most rewarding experiences of my life. It is every teachers dream come true!

Some of the names I hope to have forgotten are those of the people who hurt me by words or deeds, at different times in my life. I'm not willing to hurt myself by holding a grudge. What a powerful negative energy zapper!

I remember my former sister-in-law, but don't dwell on the uncomfortable memories, except to remember one traumatic time frame. She complained loudly how I was an uncaring spoiled brat because I would not work in their family's bakery. After putting in a day's work teaching in the classroom, and usually having evening homework to grade papers or work on projects for the following days, the physical labor of working another 5 hours/day would never have worked. For the next six months, that side of the family refused to talk with me. I definitely understood why they needed help, but I was not the solution to their problems. I felt emotionally hurt and pained by their unreasonable expectations to ask/tell me to work those hours every day. When the marriage ended, so did the strong memory of their other acts of selfishness.

While writing this chapter, I've tried to recall the names of some of the nasty people who have traveled along my path, but I can't remember most of them. Good for me! The names were attached to emotionally powerful situations. I have discarded those names from my memory. I'll continue to work on clearing out the memory of more of those people with the hurtful situations, to enable myself to let go of the unnecessary stress. I don't have any place for such negativity in my life.

Researchers tell us how people with a low sense of self worth are more likely to suffer from memory loss as they age. Self-esteem is self-respect and self-confidence, and they can be enhanced. It takes purposeful, mindful action with ongoing conscious awareness to be positive and accepting.

Healing Journal

This is a guide to self-improvement.

Check off what you did this week. In your personal healing journal (in a notebook or on a computer), add to the list on a daily basis.

_____1. Focused on doing positive things then praised myself for the success.

_____2. Did things I love doing.

_____3. Associated with people who supported me.

_____4. Listened to my gut feelings, my inner voice.

_____5. I was brave. I kept moving and working toward my goal.

_____6. Looked in the mirror and praised what I saw. Hugged myself.

_____7. Did nice things for myself that didn't cost money.

_____8. Supported and celebrated myself. Proudly patted myself on the back.

I recommend reading or listening to the audio book of "The Four Agreements: A Practical Guide to Personal Freedom" by Don Miguel Ruiz (published by Amber-Allen).

Self-limiting beliefs can hold you back. Did you say, "I couldn't do that! The boss wouldn't like it," or "I cannot buy that, she will get upset if I spend the money?" or "Oh no, it wouldn't be right, I can't do that! What will people think of me?" The book explains the idea of just because you did it one way in the past, does not mean you have to continue doing it the same way now.

The Four Agreements are:
1. Be impeccable with your word.
2. Don't take anything personally.
3. Don't make assumptions.
4. Always do your best.

There is now a fifth agreement from a later edition:
5. Be skeptical

3

When Did I Get Old?

We begin to age at birth, eagerly anticipating reaching the age of sixteen in order to drive, then the age of eighteen to vote, followed by the big powerful one of age twenty-one, when we finally become an independent adult. Such is the race to become a grown-up, an adult!

Later, we don't know whether to be excited or apprehensive about telling people our true age. Are we living fully or living with limits? Let's be proud of the insight aging has brought to us. Silver sages have bragging rights to reveal their real age.

One thing is certain: we are always aging. Living longer brings many more challenges than we can imagine. A paraphrase of the serenity poem demonstrates the way our friendships change:

God grant us the senility to forget the people we didn't like, the good fortune to run into the ones we do like, and the eyesight to tell the difference.

It is extremely important to have friends, especially esteemed friends. I used to gravitate to older, more mature friends. After my son was born, I wanted to be with families who had children the same age as my son. As a thirty nine year old new mom, I was in a different stage of life than were my previous friends. They were well past the baby phases. Then, my co-workers, who were interesting, smart, and more on my level, seem to be younger and younger. As we know, employers like to hire young people for their bright moldable minds, lower starting salary, and beautifully fresh appearances. At least we were able to be friends at work who enjoyed talking with each other and sharing thoughts and ideas.

Along came confusing talk of retirement. At this stage, I wanted to be with people my own age to level the playing field, and yet I wanted to spend time with younger people to keep pace with the modern world. Retirement was off my radar screen. I wanted to be with a variety of people of all ages and stages of life.

The big question here is, When did I get old? Was it when my son had so many birthdays that I was not able to pretend to be a young mom? It definitely was a part of aging. Was menopause the big event that made me old? It was becoming medically and physically noticeable. No doubt about it, I was aging. No more hiding it.

Was it when I stopped dying my hair because it was such a mess to apply the coloring and to cope with the awful smells? Is that when I became old, with the obvious gray hair?

One evening I spilled some dark brown hair dye on the light gray carpeting between the bathroom and bedroom. After scrubbing, rubbing, using carpet cleaning products and getting a quote for replacing the carpeting, I decided to let the real me out of the box of hair dye!

Gray hair always symbolized the frightful stage of development known as aging. After months of letting the silver gray hair grow out and getting used to the color, I found it a little easier to accept me in the mirror. Salt and pepper colored hair does not sentence me to a crime of being old. Let's change such outdated thinking, to start fresh to believe gray hair symbolizes the years of experience that came from years of gaining wisdom.

Maybe I became old when my sixty-something boss criticized me for incorrectly balancing his financial business books. He said the way I had been taught was so old-fashioned, those ways had become obsolete. Sorry, old man! In a somewhat calm manner, I reminded him about the classes I had taken in bookkeeping to learn Excel, just two years before our discussion. I was using updated computer methods, not his old-fashioned paper checkbook balancing methods.

I knew the procedures were correct, yet I felt offended at his tone and accusations. He reviewed the records at least once a month and now realized they were computer generated? He owned and ran the business, so I changed everything back to his old familiar ways. Silver sages have a dreadful reputation for being inflexible. It is usually due to a lack of understanding of our good judgment, which comes from years of experience, or someone being obviously discriminating! Or, we are being stubborn!

After having foot surgery to remove arthritis problems, I had to wear comfy, solid, sturdy shoes. Velcro closing or tie athletic style shoes are the most comfortable shoes I've ever worn. It took time to accept wearing unfashionable shoes, even though I bought white, black, and tan to try to stay somewhat stylish, in colors to match my outfits. Oh no, I'm wearing old lady shoes!

Maybe I started believing I was getting old when several physical wear and tear problems, definitely not young people's problems, presented themselves. One of the most difficult is trying to save my teeth due to periodontal problems. The complicated dental work is painful, time consuming, very expensive, and unending. I am aging, but those problems don't make me a poster woman for being old. I'm changing physically and mentally!

My mom died at age fifty-five from cancer. I did not have the opportunity to experience her senior aging, so I don't have a comparison as to what she was like at my age. She was never considered old. Dad died from natural aging at age ninety-two. He was a healthy man until his mid-eighties, when his body started to break down. Dad was bedridden, mostly bald, not very communicative, and generally seemed old due to his chronological age coupled with his declining physical abilities. For me, as an only child, sibling comparisons don't exist. Maybe I'll be old like Dad, when I can't take care of myself anymore.

Little by little, the aging process affects the eyes, the ears, hair, and more. Then the body can require a variety of medications. We really need to keep alert and organized as much as possible to follow the entanglement of medical insurance requirements, an ongoing schedule of doctors' appointments, and the need to take medications in a timely manner.

Aging can mean loneliness with some lack of mobility. Seniors can face those truths as long as they still have personal freedom, opportunities to gain more wisdom, self-confidence, and enjoy life in their own way. Let's not forget about privileges such as AARP discounts and neighborhood senior discounts. Men might not look me over any longer, but they do open doors for me!

With age comes an understanding of the way things were, the way they are, and the way they could be. One of the good things about aging, is knowing we don't lose all of those other ages we have experienced. That is an important wisdom of aging! All along the aging path, we have dreaded getting old. Becoming a silver sage can and should be rewarding. I appreciate my independence and control over decision-making. I want to be treated with the respect that should be given to an adult, of any age.

When are children considered adults? It's not just a simple matter of counting the chronological age, but accepting responsibility for self and others. Maybe getting old is no longer accepting responsibility for others. Yes, I'm on my way to getting old! It's time for me to take care of me, along with experiencing the rewards of others doing for me.

I don't know when I will declare myself old. Right now, I don't see myself as old, so I am not old! Aging, yes! Old, no!

Recently, I experienced the uncomfortable unfairness of ageism. People kept expecting me to be able to do less. When was I going to be ready to yell, "Uncle! I give up." Soon I learned to appreciate some of the help, like the pharmacist carefully explaining refills along with new medications.

Because I have always been very independent and have done things for myself, at first I resented it when the bagger at the grocery store asked to help me to the car with my groceries. My confidence returned after I heard him offer help to almost everyone. Saying yes to the next offer of help was a happy, rewarding experience.

I also recognize some situations when I'm not quite on top of my game, admitting I do need help. Sometimes, I can't catch a can as it is falling down, so I push it with my foot up against the shelving to keep the floor safe for other shoppers. It's better than feeling frustrated by not being able to pick it up to reshelf it, or by not finding someone to restock it for me. Problem solved!

There is an expectation that aging means not paying attention, which causes numerous problems. Sometimes, not listening saves us when we are not interested in the subject matter. Just tune it out. All ages use the technique of ignoring others, so why not seniors?

It took quite a few years for me to accept the truth about not being able to concentrate on two or three things at once anymore. Occasionally, it's hard enough to continue concentrating on one thing at a time. Recently, I put a small box of noodles with chicken, into the microwave, as directed. After bringing in our newspaper and a stack of mail from the mailbox across the driveway, I returned to the kitchen, feeling scared as I smelled smoke and saw it filling the house. The microwave was a mess. The food in the container had spilled onto the rotating dish and the sidewalls. The fire was small, but food and liquids were burning.

At first, I became upset that I was "losing it" by not paying attention to the directions. Had my mind been on the mail when it should have been on the cooking? As a way to validate what happened, I cleaned up the whole sticky, smelly mess, then concentrated on reading the directions again. I actually had done everything according to package directions. It wasn't me flaking out due to age; the product had not been packaged correctly.

Only then could I gain the confidence "to get off my own back" with self-criticism. I was paying attention! My natural reaction is to resent aging when I lose confidence in myself. It's a fearful, complex adjustment!

Maturing is a process to envy, but aging is not. One of the most difficult parts is forgiving yourself for the past. I would not want to live my life, or any part of it, over again. Oh sure, hindsight is a wonderful thing. If I knew then, what I know now . . .

But I didn't know more. I was as wise as I was able to be at those various stages. Aging is a full time job! I made those decisions using all the wisdom I had available to me at the time. Many people suffer a lifetime of not being willing to forgive parents for imperfections. If our parents knew more at the time of their so called mistakes, they would not have made those alleged errors in judgment.

So this is me today. I'm not old!
I know it's better to be over the hill than under it!

Who is the elder? We enter the "becoming older" stage of life then morph into "being old." I'm positioned between getting old and being old. Let's not count the days. Let's make the days count!

The question before me now that I'm getting older
Is not how to be dead.
I know that from enough practice.
How can I be alive?

4

Who Am I?

During the 1960s and 1970s, there was a big push for young people to dig deep into their souls to answer the question "Who am I?" My friends and I would talk for hours trying to figure it out. How frustrating and aggravating, none of us ever came up with answers. Eventually we moved on with our lives, concentrating on other things like family dynamics and careers.

As a silver sage, I am once again asking, "Who am I?" This time, the answer is based on many more years of living. I want to find myself, to discover who I am now, along with what I really want. Setting myself up for success by visualizing my positive goals has become a major daily objective for me, while taking one day at a time.

Who am I today? I am a combination of my work positions, social status, life experiences, thoughts, ego, relationships, my soul, and everything else about me. This is who I was meant to be.

Life isn't about finding yourself. Life is about creating yourself. - George Bernard Shaw

Is my identity based on my worth in the business world, or the caliber of my current friendships, or buying designer clothing, or on the size of my house? Many people use these as measures to identify a person while judging his or her value. Am I perceived to be less worthy because I never vacationed in Europe or because I drive a Honda?

My admiration for the real thing does not require me to own designer handbags, watches, or shoes. A logo of authenticity does not impress me unless it's on an original artistic masterpiece.

Oscar Wilde once said,
"Be yourself; everyone else is already taken."

I've spent my life trying to please other people. How could I possibly have known who I was if I was working hard to be bits and pieces of what others wanted me to be? I really believed others knew what was best for me. Accepting their magical insights never made me a better person. It's going to take time and practice to stop making people pleasing a top priority.

I want to improve as an individual set up for success. I want to find my inner self, to love myself just as I am, while doing it my way. I can and do find ways to be proud of myself without needing validation from others. However, praise with compliments are always welcomed!

The big news for silver sages is we can find our self-worth in order to love ourselves, without caring about how other people perceive us. As long as we aren't hurting anyone, being an original is better than being a clone. Those old rules about fitting in by being the same as everyone else don't apply anymore.

The most popular singing group, The Beatles, changed the course of music. To avoid admitting why they were not extra special to me, I always nodded in agreement and smiled when a discussion included their greatness. Yes, I listened to their music, but I never became spastic over their musical performances.

This year, I attended a tribute to the Beatles at a performing arts center. It was an enjoyable evening with music and friends. Part of me was expecting to enjoy the music, while another side expected me to have the same, somewhat neutral attitude from the past. Who am I today regarding my appreciation of music from the past? The musical talents of the performers on stage were admirable. My interest in the tunes and words has not changed. Some things don't change with aging. When it comes to the Beatles, I remain constant in my middle of the road appreciation of their music.

Perhaps my enjoyment did not grow because I like original performers, not impersonators. To find out how happy I can be as a listener and singer, give me Elvis Presley!

A job coach once told me to always dress the part to impress interviewers. If I wanted a management job, then I should buy fashionable shoes, designer suits with stylish blouses, and a fine leather handbag for interviews. Dressing for success required getting a manicure and pedicure, along with having my hair freshly styled the day of the interview. The coach also said to remember to take deep breaths and, most important, to be myself. If I dressed for success, interviewers would assume that I had been in a business position of a certain stature.

There is a lot to be said for the idea that appearances make the person. However, I laugh every time I think about such costly professional clothing, along with acting advice. For the interview, I did buy some business clothes without breaking the bank, and it was good for me to relax as much as possible by breathing deeply, but inconspicuously. The job coach gave me several pieces of advice on how to change myself, then over and over reminded me to "Be yourself!" That's my question, who am I? Who is the real me? Life can be perplexing!

A teacher once commented about introductions at elementary school entrances. Moms introduce themselves by saying their child's name first, such as "Hi, I'm Hal's mom, Marcia." She admonished the parents attending the meeting, saying parents have to learn right away to be identified as individuals. Turn it around and say, "Hi, I'm Marcia. My son is Hal." I'm me, by my name, not my title of mom, or wife, or . . .

I look for happiness by gravitating toward people, places and things that give me pleasure. Something as simple as hunting all over the house to find a lost store receipt, only to discover it in the bag, is a victory, which can make me feel happy. I search out and recognize the path of happiness to make my life more meaningful, more fulfilling.

As a kid, I enjoyed helping people. I remember offering to lend a hand to a neighbor with her groceries, along with helping her to cook dinner. When I'm in teaching/training mode or donating clothing to the homeless or helping a baby pick up a dropped toy, I feel happy. I am my smile!

The ultimate happiness is receiving compliments, especially from others. I feel self-conscious and shy, but I sure do enjoy them! Doesn't everyone? Knowing the joy of receiving compliments makes me wonder why I can give others permission to give me compliments but don't give myself approval to accept praise from myself? Onward to upgrading my life with more positive changes!

I am a woman who likes to sing a variety of songs. I wish I could sing big, bold, powerful songs like "Climb Every

Mountain." I long to be a singer, but I don't have the talent. It is sometimes embarrassing for me to hear myself singing in the shower, but I enjoy it, so I continue belting out those tunes. Sometimes I snore loud enough to jar myself awake during the night. Not the most appealing sound, but it is the natural me!

Life becomes more meaningful every time I forgive myself with acceptance, support, and trust. Less of my worrying comes from feeling powerless, like a Howdy Doody puppet being controlled by someone else. I don't sweat the small stuff as much as I used to. Having been an uptight perfectionist, I know the pain and suffering from migraine headaches. If guests in my house don't like me because the corners of my bathroom floor are dirty, so be it. I don't want to work hard to have a perfectly sterile house. Been there, done that!

In narrowing down how we are all special due to our feelings and life experiences, we can answer the question "Who am I?" The answer might change tomorrow with the living we do today and tomorrow. Progress can be rewarding.

Some people find it necessary to call us names, such as spry old lady, perky grandma, dear frail grandpa, or even youngster. Do people give us tag names so they can take us less seriously because we have silver hair? I call those cutesy names "disrespect." Instead of judging me, call me by my name or just talk, omitting the need for a name or aging description. I wish I could find my sense of humor around those names. Most senior sages agree, they can use a description word about themselves such as "old," but you can't!

This may sound somewhat silly (I can be silly if I'm feeling silly) to say—I recognize I am who I was, who I am now, and who I will be tomorrow.

Personal Journal:

Feelings are emotions, sensitivities, a spirit, moods, reactions, senses, beliefs, concerns, intuition, gut reactions, and all that can be bundled together under the heading of "My feelings are who I am." If anyone tells you not to feel that way, run—don't walk, run away from the person. What they are really saying is don't be your real self.

It is healthy to feel your feelings from the private perspective of your emotions along with your bodily reactions. Feelings are not right or wrong. They are not gender or age specific.

Feelings are who you are, your inner self. Many people find it difficult to understand words that convey feelings. Included in this chapter is a list of feeling words. If you want a much larger list, look up more feeling words at http://eqi.org/fw.htm

Here is a way to start getting in touch with your feelings, discovering the real you. Read over the list of positive feeling words (Table 1), and select one that closely describes how you felt during a recent experience.

How did your body react? What were your physical sensations from eyes to your fingers to your feet? What were you thinking? What did you do?

Example: Feeling Proud

I felt proud when:

_____
_____
_____

My body reacted:

_____
_____
_____

I did the following:

_____
_____
_____

At another time, a calm and quiet time, read over the attached list of negative feeling words (Table 2). Pick a negative feeling word to describe how you felt recently in a specific situation.

How did your body react? What were your physical sensations from your eyes to your fingers to your feet? What were you thinking? What did you do?

Example: Feeling Anger

    I became so angry that I:

_____
_____
_____
_____

    My body reacted:

_____
_____
_____

    I knew that I had to either fight or:

_____
_____
_____

Repeat the process frequently to become familiar with recognizing and expressing your feelings. Use this exercise often to better understand the real you.

Table 1: Positive Feeling Words
Pleasant Feelings

understanding	great	free	secure
confident	joyous	calm	fascinated
reliable	lucky	loving	thrilled
important	delighted	relaxed	considerate
kind	fortunate	bright	sensitive
alive	sympathetic	reassured	important
playful	thankful	content	eager
satisfied	interested	comfortable	comforted
glad	challenged	excited	inspired
cheerful	bold	sure	enthusiastic
hopeful	comforted	strong	curious
loved	engrossed	dynamic	challenged

Table 2: Negative Feeling Words

Difficult/Unpleasant Feelings

angry	depressed	confused	helpless
irritated	powerless	disgusting	aggressive
enraged	disappointed	dominated	alone
hostile	discouraged	provoked	pessimistic
insulting	ashamed	indecisive	fatigued
lost	resentful	perplexed	useless
annoyed	diminished	appalled	inferior
upset	doubtful	hesitant	vulnerable
restless	dissatisfied	shy	empty
unpleasant	anxious	bored	forced
offensive	tearful	disillusioned	worked up
bitter	worked up	unbelieving	uneasy
tense	sulky	skeptical	frustrated

5

Aging Is a Full Time Job

Like the bumper sticker says:
This is the oldest I've ever been!

Passionate excitement is generated over the changing advances made by babies, but the backward movement sometimes experienced by seniors provokes fear. From birth to death, people are constantly aging as they are changing. Aging is a full time job.

Mom's family was always business oriented. At one time or another, everyone in her family owned a business. Dad's family was more artistic. His siblings were good at woodworking, sewing, sign painting, designing movie sets, drafting, and so on. I inherited a sense of creativity with an instinct for being a business owner!

I always wanted to be my own boss along with owning a business. To me, running my own railroad, as was the expression in the 1960s, sounded intriguing, creative, and profitable. How special to be able to manage employees, make business decisions, as well as helping others. And working hard without a pay ceiling — oh, it all sounded wonderful! I was a teacher for seventeen years, which meant being my own boss in the classroom, but being under the rules of the school, the school district, the state, and the parents. Well, not completely my own boss!

Then my son was born, which gave me the opportunity to resign from the school system. My husband and I intended for me to be a stay at home mom with our son, in addition to having more children.

When staying at home didn't work financially, I decided to follow the family heritage by starting my own business. The Cleaning Lady was an interesting business, easy to get started, with low expenses. Unfortunately, my employees didn't stick around long enough to allow me to build a following. After a year, I ended up cleaning all the houses myself. I was the boss! If you own your business, be prepared to do everything yourself.

It seemed like all of a sudden I was in my mid forties and definitely feeling some physical midlife changes. Cleaning houses certainly was not my idea of following my bliss. The business was physically draining for this aging, full time caretaker of a preschooler. I had other business adventures, like teaching "Mommy and Me" classes and "feelings" workshops, a home-based bookkeeping business, and more.

In between the self-employment business adventures, I looked for jobs with financial security, by going back to the frustrating job search world with its age and gender discrimination. The games known as office politics left me feeling uncomfortable, unhappy and out of step since I've never been a game player. I felt tortured just by getting dressed to attend job fairs. I called them Job Unfairs! Young attendees received a lot of attention, fuss, and encouragement. Those my age or older, were asked to submit resumes. Did someone tell me life isn't fair? I missed those lessons.

I wasn't meant to work at home; in addition to being my own boss, but I sure learned a lot about businesses while learning even more about myself. I give myself credit for striking out on my own to support my family. Finding my way in the job world was such a disturbing ongoing trauma. It seemed as though it would never end. Every business is unique, every work situation is special. These individual differences made each business interesting, but I never found my happiness. I'm proud of myself for staying the course to follow job leads. Never giving up hope was a key attitude.

That's all, folks! This is called forced retirement. The boss came into my office 15 minutes before closing, on a Friday, to say, "Sorry. After seven years, I have to let you go. The business slow down doesn't warrant my having an office manager. "

I became a confused, lost soul. What was he saying? What about my lifelong decision to work forever? Somehow, in a protective mental and emotional fog, I packed my belongings, while he looked at each and every thing I touched. I left the office, never to go back to the business complex again. I had been downsized enough in my second career of being under employed to know when the end was the end.

Retired people discuss how days just fly by. They don't have time to get much done. It's true! Imagine doing whatever you want, whenever you want to do it - the schedule of the retired person. Scheduling doctor's appointments is so much easier when you don't have to squeeze them in at lunchtime or leave work early, or arrive late to the office. Admitting the timing was due to a doctor's appointment, made me feel like a child who had to account for her actions. Ahhh, the privacy! Work is an invasion of privacy! Reality check--being able to pay bills is a great motivator to work while following the rules.

No more traumas from job competition—what a dream! Is it a reality? Time will tell.

Right now, I can be true to myself. I never planned for or expected to retire. Working is all I had known since age eight when I worked in my parents' ladies and children's clothing store. It took all these years to recognize just how many times I had been under employed since leaving teaching. Hindsight shows how I had dreams with goals that those jobs never could fulfill. I was not able to use my intelligence, creativity, or capabilities on those various worker bee jobs. I wasn't able to be true to myself. My goal was to find a second career, but I had to do, what I had to do. I am always conscientious, along with being overly responsible. That's who I am!

If we keep dreaming, things have a way of working out when we least expect it, in a manner we never expected. That's one of the real values of not being young anymore. I recognize how each situation gave me the knowledge, as well as the skills needed to move toward a happier life. Becoming a silver sage has taught me there is some good in every situation.

Today is special!

One summer, I attended a local fun and educational, writing/psychology class. We had to write a short description of everyone in the class, according to certain guidelines. For each person, write what animal they represent, what color, plus more. Most of my peers wrote about my being a prancing horse, tall in stature, sitting upright in the chair, quietly looking down my nose at others, and thinking I was better than they are. What a shock! Obviously, the consensus hit shy me quite deeply. Forty years later, I still remember those judgments. Am I now like a grand, pretentious, prancing mare?

With which animal do you identify? Write it in your personal journal. Use sights and sounds to describe the surroundings.

I have always given off a façade of competence, coupled with strong self-confidence, but inside I was a scared, shy girl afraid of too many things. Not at all like a proud prancing horse, except to recognize that I am 5'9" tall.

There is an old expression: What you see is what you get. What you see is not always, or even usually, the true inner person. If I'm not willing to be true to myself, others will judge me by the face I present to them. I had a manager who reminded me of a ram. It was disturbing to realize how I let him ram into me on so many occasions because of the fear of losing my job. What happened in the end? Business kept slowing down, plus there was a recession, leading to my being downsized out of the job!

If I ruled the world, I'd mandate counseling for every person at crucial stages of life. All ninth and twelfth graders could benefit from meetings with a psychologist who specializes in their age groups.

Couples should see a specialist before marrying, before and after children are born, before divorcing, and other stressful times in life.

Another important time is when someone significant dies. All over eaters, smokers, drinkers, and drug addicts could benefit from addiction counseling. Job changers would benefit from job coaching as often as needed. The midlife crises would go much smoother with outside therapy. Talking along with writing about it helps to ease the pressures and stresses.

What about geriatric counseling? So few people are willing to specialize in counseling seniors, which leaves senior sages to struggle alone. This is a unique stage of development. For most people, facing fears of the unknown is scary, so they stop themselves from asking for help. We are a distinctive blend of all our stages of life. Updating our thinking and acting is essential to moving forward. A geriatric specialist can be a lifesaver. A counselor, psychologist, psychiatrist, or whatever specialist you choose to find, could be your mental and emotional roto-rooter, or clean out and clean up person. Create a clear and clean path for the new perceptions to come in.

My geriatric psychologist has helped me through changes I recently experienced. Talking with him has been lifesaving. I can better understand my present life and how past events have led me to where I am today. Now it is time to move forward on the senior path of changes.

Reboot the brain, to update the memory, to verify how everything is changing! I asked my credit union to update my account. I didn't realize I never arranged for my son to use my account if I became incapacitated. He was on the account only as the beneficiary. Every couple of years, update and verify your status with all credit cards, bank accounts, life insurance policies, and homeowners and car insurance. Those accounts age too.

What are the challenges to be a successful retiree? Because I was not expecting to stop working, I'm learning now to set reasonable goals. Living in the present is very important. In the past, my identity was always with my job title. The first thing we ask a new acquaintance is, "What do you do?" Retiring means giving up that job identity and reinventing a new positive identity with a new, flexible daily schedule.

Much to my amazing delight, I do not miss the work, but I do miss the daily structure of being busy, feeling needed, and mostly of the office friendships. Of course, not having a paycheck is quite a shock requiring planning on a "forever" basis. One of the joys of leaving the control of the job environment includes the freedom and control of never having to worry about counting benefits to avoid using up too many vacation or sick days.

After allowing a fair amount of time to mourn about my aging, which meant possibly retiring, I returned to my love of creative writing. My new job is being a personal manager. I manage me on a full time basis. I run my own railroad! I'm the boss of me, the person in charge of all the facets of my life. I don't have to account to anyone. It's always been up to me to find and follow my bliss by searching for answers within me. Now is the time to listen to my inner self. In the past, this kind of "being my own boss" would never have been on my radar screen.

What a dream come true! By knowing the future is mine, I appreciate the goodness in my life!

> *You know, by the time you reach my age, you've made plenty of mistakes, if you've lived your life properly.* **– Ronald Reagan**

Part Two: *Encouragement*

6

I Wish, I Wish, I Wish

Setting goals is challenging. Having wishes come true is super exciting. Simplify life by concentrating on carefully making plans, and then on implementing them. I can look at my wish list, take out the still relevant wishes, and work to make them come true. Many of the old wishes don't apply anymore. That's inspiring too!

What have I wanted for a very long time? Here is today's list. DONE means I did achieve it, but it is an ongoing project. Which ones are your wishes too?

1. Give my body and mind the opportunity to wake me up in the morning. No alarm or clock radio jarring me awake. DONE!

2. Be my own personal decision maker. Be my own personal manager. Be my own boss. DONE!

3. Take advantage of senior discounts at restaurants and ask for discounts everywhere. DONE!

4. Keep in mind that forgetting isn't a crime. I can remember the good things and forget the useless bits

and pieces. Then if necessary, I can still blame it on having a senior moment. DONE!

5. Look in the mirror and accept myself. That's me, and that's the way I am. Almost DONE!

6. Quit holding my stomach in, when in public. DONE!

7. Get plenty of healthy exercise — jumping to conclusions, pushing my luck, and dodging telemarketers! DONE!

I want to have a growing list for tomorrow, to make progress in my life as I make more wishes come true today.

On the active wish list are:
1. Feeling secure in recognizing an abundance of finances and good health to give me a quality of life and not just a quantity of life.

2. Knowing and accepting who I really am as I continue to change and improve.

3. Accomplishing artistic endeavors, such as creative writing.

4. Thinking positively, acting confidently, being optimistic.

5. Accepting my limitations and improving my strengths.

6. Smiling and laughing every day.

7. Wishing for more positive wishes.

Many how-to books guide us on the path to making our wishes come true. If you believe in spells, mantras, repetition, or good luck charms, use them or whatever makes you feel comfortable. Wishing is often accompanied by wishing wells or a focus on birthday candles and products such as weight-loss pills.

The power of positive thinking, along with lots of hard concentration work and constant practice are the best tools. A wish is for a dream to come true. Intending to do something isn't enough. To succeed, it is necessary to concentrate fully while positively knowing a successful outcome is here. Pursue the dream daily to invite a wish to come true.

I have been wishing for many years to be almost as thin as a model. Just wanting it to be so or intending it to be so isn't enough. Taking off the extra weight as well as keeping it off requires a full time, positive attitude and super powerful, consistent determination.

My written wish list noticeably does not include material objects. Keeping up with the Joneses and buying every new product, were never a part of my wish list. Following the latest, ever changing fashions in work or in life is spiritual and intellectual suicide. I'm a practical Capricorn who considers the common sense of purchasing the product rather than buying it just to say I have it. Being so practical doesn't give my family and friends much leeway for holiday or birthday gifts, so I frequently get things I won't use. I do understand this difficult gift giving dilemma.

I'm not a collector of objects. I suggest gifts of pampering like spa type body lotion, a manicure, pedicure, or a massage. Also, tickets to a musical, a psychic reading, a house-cleaning service, or anything that's useful and practical to make my life easier and happier. This year for Mother's Day, my son bought a new set of sharp kitchen knives. They sure make cooking easier! Such a very useful and appreciated gift! Have you told your family and friends what kind of gifts you would like?

By being sensible, I have avoided doing anything really silly. Yes, I have a few regrets, but none for silly decisions or actions. No tattoos, eating bugs, singing silly loud songs in an elevator, or using the men's room at a concert. I've called myself silly (in a flippant way) for expecting perfection, such as "silly me" expected the sales representative to call on Saturday when he said he would. Or "silly me" expected the recliner couch footrest to work after it had been fixed for the third time. Now I know how silly can be a great adventure for silver sages. Break out of the box and be silly! Being mature does not have to mean being serious and sullen all the time.

Retrospection provides an interesting view of earlier times. The past sums up who I am today, so it is probably best I did not change my mind along the way. I wouldn't be me! This is a sample of some of the decisions that led me to these wishes.

► I wish I had put myself first instead of focusing attention on others. Giving is loving. On numerous occasions, I forgot about giving to myself, loving myself. It's doubly hard for my generation of women who were taught to be nurturers.

► I wish I had taken the effort to figure out what I wanted and who I was, more often in the past. For example, when people asked where I wanted to go for dinner, I answered as though I was a character from the movie Marty. My mind would freeze, leaving me to ask where they wanted to go.

► I wish I had the confidence to know what a remarkable woman I've always been. Doesn't every man and woman have this wish? We can't go back, can't rewind time, but we can start over from here.

► I wish the impossible were possible. I'd be shorter, thinner, have blue eyes, enjoy physical exercise, sing while cleaning the toilets. I would be rich enough to buy clothing and medicine for orphans all over the world. If only there were coupons for all those things, I'd be out there shopping right now!

Ahhh, to face reality as it is, along with putting in the time and effort to attract wishes to improve reality!

Just do it!

Healing Journal:

Writing is healing. Now it's your turn to write your wish list. Just write. There is no minimum or maximum length to a wish list. It's private.

What do you wish you had done differently in the past?

_____

_____

_____

_____

What do you want to change for the present and the future?

_____

_____

_____

_____

7

Endings Are Beginnings

Whenever something ends, a beginning is waiting in the wings. When the moon turns day into evening, sunshine will follow again with a new day.

One of the most overwhelming endings in my life came just six months after marriage, my first husband left me. I told him I might be pregnant. He stalled in taking responsibility to use birth control when my doctor told me to stop using the pill due to migraine headaches.

One Friday evening, when he came home from work late, as was usual every Friday night, I decided to surprise him. I traced around my left foot, then my right, on several pieces of white paper. I cut out the feet and placed them in alternating order as though someone had walked from the front door, through the dining area, down the hall, and into the bedroom. The cut out feet led exactly to me in bed!

He came home around midnight, fiddled with the keys in the door, then turned on the light. After several minutes of quiet, while I was about to burst from my mounting excitement, I heard him walking into the bedroom. He asked if I was awake enough to go into the living room to talk. He said the paper feet were really cute. He appreciated them.

The request to talk caught me completely off guard. I sat on the couch, waiting impatiently for him to talk.

He said our marriage was not working out for him! This was coming on for quite a while, he had been unhappy for months. What? We had been dating for three years and married for only six months. As a new business owner, he couldn't cope with my asking so much of him, in addition to his time. He had to spend days and evenings building his company, which was only a year old.

Also, he had to spend weekend time with his brother in their new business partnership of only nine months. How unbelievable, we were newlyweds! I asked for too much by wanting to talk on the phone every evening, and spend time together at least one weekend evening? What if I was pregnant? He said he didn't want a baby at this time, but would help to support the baby when his businesses grew enough for him to take profits.

First, there was a numbing silence. Then crash, bang, kaboom were the mental sounds of my world coming to an end! Nothing was real, not the words, not the room, nothing!

He slept on the couch for a couple of hours, took some of his belongs, and left early in the morning. Everything else was removed from the apartment the next week, during the day while I was teaching.

A few days later, the doctor gave me a shot, not knowing if my body would react by doing nothing, or aborting if I was pregnant. Back then, it was too early to confirm pregnancy. I walked around in a fog, nothing was real. A week later, the Doctor said the current pregnancy test came back as negative. I never knew what had really happened.

What a heartbreaking siege of endings! It was a complicated and emotionally draining time for me.

My brother-in-law called a couple of times to try to find out whether I was pregnant. We had a loving relationship, but I would not discuss it with him. None of us ever talked again. The divorce papers did not include child support, so they had their answers for the end of the marriage along with the end of our story. One of the great things about aging is how the powerful punch from something that emotional has a way of dissipating after years of beginnings taking over. There is still pain, a lot of emotional pain from being abandoned.

As much as I wanted a baby, my chance was gone. I couldn't continue to dwell on the rejection, the anguish, or the humiliation. Teachers weren't paid during the summer months. My husband said his two start-up businesses would support us during the summer months of no teacher's pay, so saving money wasn't necessary. We needed to live day by day during this first year of marriage.

It was June, neither business was yielding a profit, and my husband wasn't returning my phone calls. No time to grieve! I had to find a summer job, super fast.

Fortunately, I found two part time jobs to support myself during the summer. I had to move beyond the marriage, accept we wouldn't make it to the future together, plus find new ways to survive. Talk about a powerful need for a new beginning. Whew! The future really meant living for today. Tomorrow will take care of tomorrow. Teachers plan ahead for classroom hours, days, weeks, and months. Living one day at a time was new to me.

As I moved through the summer in a daze of existence and survival, my life started to take shape. School started in September, which gave me some resemblance of my former life. When the beginnings take over, the door opens to let the future in.

There comes a point in your life when you realize who matters, who never did, who won't anymore, and who always will.

Death is one of the most dramatic endings we can experience. Divorce is the death of a relationship. Being down sized out of a job is the death of the job.

A few years ago, I began to accept physical death as an ending when, given enough time and distance, will lead to a new beginning. This realization brings a resolve to keep good memories active while triggering new beginnings.

Within an eighteen-month time span, eleven special people died. They were cousins, uncles, aunts, friends, my second husband, and my dad. Letting go is so difficult. It is a huge mission to make sense of a loved one not being here anymore. Reliving memories, being critical of myself for not doing more, mourning losses, and coming to terms with my own mortality were the realities that had to be faced. They were all a part of the process of getting ready for new beginnings without each of those loved ones. Some people recognize new starts but don't connect them with the endings making them possible. I never did before becoming a senior sage and experiencing so many losses.

Those people had been a buffer between mortality and me. When that buffer generation ended, I was pushed to the front of the line. Moving up the ladder of aging is uncomfortable as well as frightening.

Take one step at a time toward new beginnings. Being the family matriarch is just a title, not a death sentence. I keep reminding myself of the reality.

I made sure my personal legal documents were in order and readily accessible for my son. The lessons from those deaths also taught me to get my life in order. It might be later than I think!

Talking about our final wishes with health care providers and the people who will take care of our ending time is challenging. I'm not afraid of being dead. I talk about it somewhat pragmatically. I am terrified of suffering for no reason. DNR: Do Not Resuscitate me!

My DNR decision is in my living will, and I have a copy of it in my wallet. I don't want tubes, needles, and bags keeping me alive. For what? If I can't have a quality life, I don't want life at all. People everywhere face the challenges of endings, then beginnings. As the world turns with these challenges and opportunities, I choose to get off if I can't be saved—DNR!

Birth is the first of what I call the three stages in our life process. Infancy through the teen years and up to age 21 is the stage of great growth and developmental advancement. Stage two is adulthood, with careers and family responsibilities, including the midlife crisis, during which we review the past to prepare for the successes of the future. Stage three is becoming a senior citizen with a need to downsize, slow down, and reinvent the self to look for new life discoveries. We do everything possible to end stage three without debilitating illnesses, dementia, or Alzheimer's. Death is the ending which gives our survivors the gift, even though it is an unkind gift, of a new beginning. Where are you on this path through the stages of development?

Time to move on to happier thoughts, like finding new passions and new bliss, especially after an ending. Not knowing your passion or purpose means you have infinite possibilities to explore. I search daily to find new interests along with new people. Some days I just want to sit on the couch to watch TV without feeling pressured to explore. That's all right too! The road to change is bumpy and can be messy, especially when we realize life is like a roll of toilet paper. The closer it gets to the end, the faster it seems to go! New beginnings require a sense of humor. Sharpen your wit! Get the laughter going!

Okay, back to serious business of being courageous. Buying a house was a someday project. Why did I keep on renting for decades? Buying was too big of an undertaking for me to accomplish on my own. When real estate was booming, I saw sale prices increase monthly and knew they would be way out of reach for me quite soon.

Then, there it was, the townhouse I wanted! It was the right size, in the right location, and at a currently affordable price. Every room needed some upgrading, but nothing is perfect.

Buying a house was an elephant of a task! Too many obstacles, too big of a project for me! When I discussed the impossible idea of buying it, my Aunt Edith and Uncle Benny offered to give me an early inheritance gift of the $3,000. I needed their boost of confidence. Also, the money for the closing costs was greatly appreciated. I had the money for the down payment and enough to do some basic upgrading. Little by little, bit by bit, I chipped away at the problems in my new adventure as a homeowner. I don't ever want to be a renter again. That phase of my life has ended. My home has given me so much pleasure during the past twelve years. I look forward to spending many more happy years here.

Even though I said I would not discuss physical problems in this book, I'm including vision problems as a story about creating new beginnings. Unclear vision led to needing reading glasses, then feeling sick with trifocals, and ended with my wearing bifocals. At the beginning of this stage in the aging process I kept saying, "I don't want those old lady bifocals," so I suffered with on-again, off-again reading glasses. My frustrations from having to adjust to those years of wearing annoying reading glasses turned into an opportunity to find the best solution. Now I keep the bifocal glasses on all the time. No more switching, no worrying about having the right glasses with me. This was a great way to relieve the stress of forgetting my glasses and of giving me a clear, new road to see in front of me.

Problems are opportunities!

8

New Age Roto-Rootering

Roto-Rootering is an investment in excellent health and happiness. Starting with the subject of good quality health, the question is, "Who is the roto-rooter medical man? Inside my head, I call my gastroenterologist, the Roto-Rooter Man. I dread seeing him to arrange for colonoscopies to inspect my tangle of a colon. This kind of examination forces the patient to joke or "lose it" just to get through the procedure, even with a nice Dr. Roto-Rooter. It is a painless exam process. Clearing out all the food from the body is best handled by preparing to live in the bathroom for several hours the night before the procedure. It is a necessary process; don't avoid it!

My most recent colonoscopy was scheduled for the day before Thanksgiving. The next available appointment was near Christmas. I didn't want to torture myself with the wait and worry.

Several people "tsk-tsked," shaking their heads, asking why I'd go through such an examination the day before a holiday. Dinner preparations were completed ahead of time for my family. Why wait and worry? The media does an excellent job of convincing the world of how the aging population has a difficult time making appropriate decisions. Remember individual differences! We are not all the same.

The day before the procedure, I rallied to gain inner confidence, knowing the timing and decisions were right for me at this time. Those well meaning friends were reacting to themselves, not to my personal situation. I shook off their questioning, trusting myself, along with changing my focus and concentration to a positive direction.

My personal history reveals I am quite a capable woman, but I'm not an island! I need people, love, support, and even to be taken care of at various times. Even capable silver sages know they deserve help. I am learning it is absolutely fine while often necessary, to ask for help. There is so much to learn about the challenging opportunities of being a silver sage. The best is yet to come!

The previous colonoscopy was five years earlier, when I was working full time. I had to deal with it alone. No one was available to drive me to the appointment. I always gave off an aura of confidence, saying it was okay, I can make the arrangements. Everything will be fine.

In the morning, the taxicab never came. I was fortunate to see my new neighbor pulling out of her parking space while I was frantically pacing the carport area, looking for the cab. She graciously granted my request to drive me to the local endoscopy center. I stressed and worried the whole time about getting a ride home. Yes, I'm the queen of worrywarts!

The nurse at the medical center called a cab, told the driver to come to the front office to walk me to the cab, then drive me home. Whew! Staying well means not allowing anything to stand in the way of getting attention to maintain good health.

This current much improved time of life eased the stress, allowing me to be confident the results would be fine. And they were fine, and I'm fine! My son took the day off work to be with me for this colonoscopy procedure, eliminating all my anxiety about getting to the medical center on my own.

Reach for the best outcome, take one day at a time, keep a positive outlook, and listen to your gut feelings. Take a deep breath for that tall order!

Ladies, let's discuss my idea of the roto-rooter techniques to clean out the personal debris to clear the path for the future. How about cleaning out your purse? I'm a tall woman, who was often told I looked more in proportion when I used a large shoulder bag. Once the shoulder pains made those bags uncomfortable, I became aware of carrying a bunch of junk no longer needed. My son was in high school at the time, but I was still carrying a "mommy bag" full of what-if bits and pieces. I don't need scissors, two pens, notebook, assorted band-aids, wipes, telephone change, and more.

Now my lightweight, soft, tan shoulder bag is a small nine inches by five inches shoulder bag with no fumble outside pockets for keys and cell phone. The new red wallet is a nice soft, small size with room to easily find all the essentials.

Never ever, carry your credit cards in your wallet! I learned an important lesson, the hard way, when my wallet was stolen along with irreplaceable family photos and all my credit cards. What a struggle to replace everything! Unfortunately, I did not have copies of the pictures. They are gone forever. Advice -- make current photocopies of the contents of your wallet. Store them in a safe place.

Carry only the credit cards or store cards you intend to use during the day. Definitely hide them somewhere in zippered areas or a closeable pocket.

Hiding feelings is a completely different roto-rooter formula. Your feelings are the unique person you are at this time. Accept what is, forgive, then go on with life. That is the roto-rooter clean out method to stop feeding and holding onto the grudge monster.

My friend was terribly hurt when her uncle did not welcome her to stay in his house after a terrible storm almost destroyed her hillside home. The grudge festered with increasing anger until my friend broke off all ties with her uncle and his side of the family. She was unable to forgive, to move forward by accepting what had happened. The issues were never discussed, never resolved. Her uncle died in the hospital, which left the anger and the grudges to be passed on to family members, pitting one side against the other. The journey to freedom is forgiveness.

This roto-rooter method of cleaning out, along with organizing, extends to both physical and mental clutter busting. The physical clutter can be from any disorganized environment with just too much stuff. Motivators tell us how to accomplish a seemingly impossible task by discussing how to eat an elephant. Take one bite at a time. Clean five objects a day, or one room per week, or whatever it takes to improve your space as well as your memory and health. Break the project down into bite size pieces.

My friend and her sister, who were obese, lived as roommates with a growing collection of everything. They were experienced hoarders. Their mom died fifteen years ago, but they were still saving her favorite hats, wall art, knickknacks, along with just about every memory piece from their beloved mom. Dad's stuff was in their garage too, as was their deceased auntie's collections of various knick-knacks. They wanted to get rid of the clutter but could not bring themselves to throw anything away.

Letting go could have freed them from some of their physical and emotional problems, but they could not do it. It required a change of mind-set, which included making a commitment to success and to avoid procrastination. They had a real clean up nightmare, which could only be solved with professional help. They waited too long to do the clutter busting on their own. The clutter caused each one to outgrow her own bedroom space. They each moved into a spare bedroom and started cluttering some more.

How long have you been keeping stuff in desk drawers, dressers, and nightstands? It's shocking to see what is in there, especially if you haven't taken everything out in the past ten years. Since I've been giving things away to charities, such as the Shelter for Battered Woman, on an annual basis, I thought I had my clutter under control. Then, I became involved in this process of using the roto-rooter method to look at each and every item to clean up the clutter.

It took several weeks to get the job done, but I dug in, to look through a couple of drawers each day.

I saved so many paper clips that I wondered if I could make a piece of artwork with them. No way!

What about the old, smaller-size casual blouses that hadn't been worn since before the start of the millennium? Gone, donated! What about those bits and pieces of memorabilia from plays, vacations, and special events? Tossed out, gone!

Reliving old memories was interesting, as was the realization that the past is gone. It's time to update, time to let go, definitely the point to move forward. With all the resulting extra space, I was able to keep the current items, in addition to some of the older memories like the gold bracelet of puffed hearts worn on the day I got married. Now you know the methods of roto-rootering. Try it; you might like it!

Seniors are known to complain about memory loss (See Chapter 2). I strive to get rid of the clutter, the worry, as well as the useless memories, to make my load lighter. Yes, it means cleaning out bookshelves, kitchen drawers, jewelry boxes, shoes, the glove compartment of the car, the garage, attic, and the sewing machine cabinet, too. I never liked to have too much stuff, clutter confused me.

I know the importance of praising myself for doing what it takes to create a contented, more manageable life. Knowing isn't enough. Action is required to promote self-esteem

When my life is in balance, I'm not obsessing over anything. I can appreciate the beauty in nature, hear every note played during a piano recital, and be grateful for the silliness of everyone's sense of humor. Laughter is the roto-rooter of the soul!

9

Attitude of Gratitude

Who said life gets easier as you get older? As I was celebrating birthdays, maturing, as well as gaining wisdom, it would have made sense for me to use all my skills to achieve an easier, more prosperous life. The real truth is that life is tough, really tough. When I was in college, Mom would quite often say, "Life is tuff, T-U-F-F." Life has its ups and downs. No matter how you spell it, life is T-U-F-F.

Eleanor Roosevelt said,
"With the new day, comes new strength and new thoughts. For that, we can be grateful."

Children are told to change their attitude, as though that was the magical way to solve problems. Children don't know the meaning of such an abstract idea. Many adults don't know what it means to change their attitude, let alone how to make those changes.

Attitude is perspective, so the purposeful changing of your point of view will change your attitude. As an only child, I went with the flow of life as it was delivered. Perhaps siblings would have made a difference. I don't know. I thought my attitude was mature, just like the adults in my life.

Adults told me I was too negative. I guess they thought it would help to change my attitude if they continued to criticize me. I took it as disapproval and reprimand reinforcing my feelings of inferiority.

Now I wish I had asked them exactly what they wanted me to do. I thought it must be true, I must be extremely negative. Looking for the up side, the positive side, the happy side, became an essential goal. If only I could change my attitude, I would have the good life! I would be so grateful to be a happy, up-beat person. What is an attitude and how do I change mine? I wanted to be perfect -- for them.

Problems are opportunities! That's how we learn our greatest lessons, get on the course to make changes, and mature. When I look back at the opportunities my problems have handed to me, I can see how I developed into the person I am now.

Eventually, I came to understand the difference between being negative versus being positive. It's an inside job, which gives feelings of satisfaction or discontent. Today is the most positive I've ever been in my life. I do look for the smiling approach to everything, from everyone. I'm grateful every time I recognize optimism in my life.

Changing to a more optimistic attitude has led me along the path to improving my self-esteem, enhancing my confidence, appreciating the good things in life, along with complimenting others and myself. I'm letting others know the unique me by making a constant effort to be true to myself.

Sometimes, peers don't like it, but as long as I'm being true to myself and not hurting anyone, I intend to stop worrying about what others think about me. How far along the path are you to gaining self-esteem? How do you feel about making changes?

Because of their many responsibilities, adults have worries with serious talks. Children have fun, play, giggle, and laugh. During my childhood, I was surrounded and influenced by adults with their hush, hush conversations and serious talks about solving problems. I heard them talking, but I never involved myself in their discussions, unless they wanted me to do something for the family. I would stay with my grandmother, Little Bubbie, or take her to the doctor, or do other things for the family. These experiences taught me to be a caring and giving person in an adult, responsible manner.

Silver sages know all about attitudes from the people in their lives. I've been on the receiving end of an inconsiderate attitude where I wanted to get physically violent with the offender. That is my polite way of saying I wanted to punch his lights out! When I was growing up, I learned boundaries!

Work was being done in my townhouse complex to tear down the thirty year old, wooden patio fences to replace them with a cement concoction. During the process, construction workers dug up half of my patio bricks, piling them in a corner. The bricks were never returned to their original positions. The property manager was insensitive to my plight until I lost patience with him. I insisted upon setting up a face-to-face meeting at my house.

During the meeting on my patio, I held firm, relating how I had waited for the promised solution for six months. Will the patio be returned to its original condition this week or next? He took a deep breath, saying he would arrange for it to be fixed the next week. I asked him if he was a man of his word. With head bowed, he softly said, "We will see." What a clear, obvious answer! The patio was finally restored after three more weeks of confrontations.

The property manager never did change his attitude; he was not a man of his word. The townhouse management company was replaced the following year due to constant complaints from homeowners. I'm so grateful I don't have to deal with that company anymore.

I was under-employed for years, working in an office where one of my co-workers was the obvious favorite. My resentment grew as I saw my high level of experiences and qualifications were not appreciated. I was torn between wanting to be friends with my co-worker and resenting her elevated approval by the head of the company. I'm grateful I maintained a cooperative attitude while keeping my patience. After several years, my persistence paid off. It did improve the daily routine in the office atmosphere. I'm thankful it worked out that my kindness succeeded; by the same token, I was able to be true to the real me. Persistence is a tough struggle, however it can bring rewards.

My life story unfolded with my being a giving person, but when I was out of step with the dynamics at work, fate took over to force me out to go on the way to more and better opportunities. What does that mean? I was downsized out of the job!

Learning never ends. No matter how much we know, there is always more to learn, especially as our society and technology continue to make enormous progress. It is important to keep up with the modern times. Learning something new every day is exciting. When contemplating buying anything new, like a microwave or computer, I'm grateful to be able to search the Internet to compare styles with prices. The computer has made my life so much easier than when I shopped store to store for the best deal. Today, it would be too exhausting for me to go to several stores to shop.

If you don't use a computer, be grateful you have the background and experiences to have taught you how to get things done without a computer.

If you can learn to use the computer, go for it! It's the most rewarding brain exercise ever invented, especially to keep senior minds active and alive.

So much to learn, so little time! Take every opportunity to show an attitude of gratitude!

**Gratitude makes sense of our past,
brings peace for today, and
creates a vision for tomorrow!**

A Gratitude Journal:

A gratitude journal is a problem solving tool to clarify thoughts, to enable us to express feelings. A gratitude journal helps me feel more appreciative of my life. Some people like fancy, leather bound books, others, yellow legal pads or notebook paper. My favorite is the very convenient computer.

Similar to writing in a private diary as children do, every night I write down three to five positive happenings from the day that made me feel cheerful and appreciate the day. By ending the day on such a positive note, I wake up feeling optimistic to enable me to look forward to a bright new day.

Here are a couple of lines for you to practice for tonight's gratitude experience. Create your own style with your own words. This is a starting place for your personal, private journal.

I am grateful for:

_____

_____

_____

_____

10

A Woman's Gotta Do
A Man's Gotta Do

I cannot control situations presented to me, but I can control my reactions to them. Some jobs have an element of high stress/low control.

Oh no, the fraud investigator is coming! That's not the way I wanted my arrival to be announced. I don't know of any child who has dreamed of growing up to be a fraud investigator. I worked for a year as an administrative assistant for an insurance company. The job of field and office auditor was traditionally held by men, but the director and I knew I could handle it. Management said I was the most qualified candidate, especially since I was already working in the premium auditing department. With such praise and encouragement showered upon me, I happily accepted the position. I needed the promotion to support my son and myself!

The title on my official business card was "Premium Auditor," but my job was really to investigate insurance fraud from high risk transportation businesses. Depending on the size of the business and other criteria, the State of California required an audit of their bookkeeping. I reviewed the books and records and wrote a report. The review caused recommended changes to insurance policies based on the paperwork the transportation company mailed to my office, or when I reviewed it during a field audit. The decision as to which, working in the office or doing a field audit, was at my discretion. As long as the financial records matched the licensing rules, then I would not recommend changes. It was an ego boost to go back to being in charge of my own schedule and workload.

Most neighborhoods in California were known to be safe, while others felt creepy and scary, especially for a woman traveling alone. The manager did not think it was necessary for me to have full time use of the company's one cell phone. Four of us were told to figure out how to share it. If the phone was available, I could check it out, as long as I returned it the same day. If I didn't have the company phone, I was instructed to use a pay phone and keep records to be reimbursed. The men in the claims department scrambled to arrive at the office first each day to get the cell phone. I did what I had to do in order to accomplish my job independently, without being a part of their game.

One day, I was lost in an area known for its many drug dealers. I drove around for some time, looking for a pay phone that seemed safe. Finally, I found two phones out in the open, without any businesses or houses nearby. I visually scouted the area, gave myself a pep talk, then dashed to the phone booth.

The first phone did not have a receiver; the other one was covered in vomit! I drove to a gas station where the attendant gave me directions, then strongly urged me to lock the car doors!

I double checked the trucking business address against my directions, as I drove up to the intimidating bars surrounding the high gates topped with wired fences. I felt threatened by the growling, barking dogs running on the building's roof. After stating my name and business at the entrance gate, an employee opened the gate that led into the complex. I was very aware of the startling, snarling sounds of the dogs just above me.

After finding my way through a security maze, I was introduced to the husky, middle-aged owner, who motioned me to sit down in front of his large, well-polished desk. He reached over to give me a firm handshake, along with a hostile gaze, which lasted just a few seconds too long. I became aware of the necessity to resume breathing again! As I felt the oxygen return to my lungs, the owner asked why I was there, interrupting his morning.

I reviewed the audit letter and our telephone conversations, reminding him about our agreement to have a meeting. He didn't reply. Instead, he took a pistol out of the desk drawer and firmly placed it on the desk, with the barrel facing me. It was a short meeting, completely without cooperation. I scurried out of there much faster than I had entered the trucking complex.

I struggled with the car keys, eventually entered my car, and drove away as calmly as possible. My mind and body had enough to do to keep me driving safely to return to my office, without thinking about the day's other appointments. As I drove back to the office, shaking and crying, I vowed to quit the job!

As a single mom, I was desperate for an income. Friends, along with co-workers, encouraged me to stick with the work, but I didn't need a lot of convincing. Most of the time it was an okay job. There were several helpful perks, such as medical insurance and a company car. Every job has its problems, which sometimes require different approaches to survive. Field auditing usually means going out to much nicer locations with most of the work completed in the office. But a woman's gotta do what a woman's gotta do!

I did find a way to stop going to those well known dangerous areas by having the information sent to my office. Problems can generate opportunities for creative ways to solve dilemmas.

I could not find another solution except to look for a different job, while doing this one to the best of my abilities. I was not being true to what I knew was best for me. The obligations of being the family provider, of doing it all alone, were intense. My inspiration came from the old Frank Sinatra song "High Hopes." The ant knows he can't move a rubber tree plant. No little ant can. But as long as he has high hopes, he will push to succeed at moving the rubber tree plant.

Sometimes we do things out of sync with being true to ourselves. Staying for a short time can have advantages. A long run at the wrong thing can wreck havoc on our lives. After making the necessary changes, the result can be an easier life, a happier life, and we question why we didn't try it sooner. Try it . . . you might like it!

The perfectionist in me has learned to be comfortable with dishes in the sink overnight when I don't want to put them in the dishwasher. Oh my, Oh my! Every now and then, I crave a yummy, greasy, unhealthy hamburger with fries and a soda. Most times, I don't feel like walking to the kitchen to answer the phone, so I screen the calls. Silly me, I can do whatever I want. I'm the boss of me!

What feelings do you want to attract in a greater quantity in your life? Feeling thankful, appreciated, joyous, fascinated? What else? Concentrate on attracting those feelings while knowing just how you will feel when they do come into your life. We all have to do what we think is in our best interest!

Start with one feeling at a time. For example, I want to bring more happiness into my life. Happiness brings an inner glow to my being, causing me to sit upright, to walk straighter, to smile, and generally, to feel more relaxed. Happiness in the form of laughter is my daily goal. I want the sudden rush of excitement, the tightening of the stomach, the laughing, the huge smiles, together with the feeling of relief when I relax.

My feelings are who I am. My feelings from all the situations I've experienced in my life make me who I am. Do you still trust the judgments of others instead of your own decisions?

**Just when the caterpillar thought the world
was over, she became butterfly!**

I relied on the judgments of others to validate my worth. No wonder my life was out of balance. As a silver sage, I recognize I must be an agent of change. I must be the change I want for myself. I continue being fully committed to making adjustments in my life by listening to myself to balance the ups and downs in my life. A woman's gotta do what a woman's gotta do!

The balancing act to have a well rounded life is a lifelong process. Look in the mirror. Who looks back at you? My eyes have always been the mirror to my soul. Most people see honest, revealing emotions in my eyes. I rarely get any privacy because of these expressive eyes! If the person looking at me is reading my body and eye language, I will know by the response. If the person asks a pertinent question about me, then I know he or she is at least reading some of the feelings from my eyes, along with my emotions. The desirable outcome is to be with someone who will listen to my answer, then respond, to balance the conversation.

In Hamlet, Shakespeare wrote:
> ***To thine own self be true.***

People throughout history have yearned for the knowledge of how to be true to themselves.

Part Three: *New Points of View*

11

What If . . .

My mom used to say, "Don't wish your life away." I don't think it is possible for a silver sage to be afraid, without wishing for the end to a fearful situation, the sooner the better. Unless you are fifty or older, especially sixty-five or older, it is difficult to understand how you face fears in such a noticeably different way than during previous stages of life.

The common worries for seniors are mostly of current and possible future poor health, physical suffering, plus not having enough money to get through the rest of life. Dying peacefully without suffering is our goal. I want to live long enough to have a quality of life, not a quantity of life.

Sometimes I ask myself what I would prefer if I could choose my end. Who knows, maybe I will have the opportunity to decide. Someday, doctors might have the power to cooperate with patients to fulfill their desires to stop the agony. I don't want to be in pain or see my loved ones suffering for me. I want a fast end to my life.

I never want to fall, whether up or down. As we age, there is a natural physical imbalance, along with a lack of coordination, and a great fear of falling. It is common to have experienced falling down a step, but stepping up, missing a step, then falling up onto the next step? It happened once to me when I was a teenager.

We lived in a two-story house with what must be Murphy's Law. Whatever we needed was always in some other place. I was rushing upstairs to get a book from my bedroom, along with trying to take two steps at a time. I stumbled and fell up a step. A few carpet brush burns hurt my legs and arms. I felt a bewildering fear during the fall. The dread of doing it again made me walk up and down the steps at a slower pace, at least for a few weeks. Young people find it easier than adults to brush off scary experiences.

Facing the fear is the only way to find the solution. If I stumbled up a step today, I'd probably take care of the immediate situation, then get help, followed by recalling it over and over at later times. Obsessing comes easily with aging, as does being a worrywart.

I heard a man in the bank sternly telling his silver sage mom to "Forget about it already!" She was angry with herself for leaving her grocery money on the kitchen counter and was afraid of not being able to buy food. Being on the receiving end of such verbal obsessing requires an eye to eye calm, patience, and reassurance about how to resolve the problem. The frustration and anger expressed by the mom at the bank are natural reactions to stress.

Psychologists explain fear as a blocked wish, often resulting in anger.

At age forty-something, I had to jump over a large, deep hole due to construction work on the parking lot outside of my office. The workers, along with my boss, encouraged me repeatedly, saying I could make the jump safely and easily. I was shaking, rigid, and overcome with panic and fear.

Feeling afraid to look yet not look, I held the strong hand of my boss, while making a successful jump. It was the only way to get to my car. I kept my thoughts on the goal of driving home.

During the night, I worried about whether I would have to jump over the construction hole again the next morning. The fear mounted. I decided on several possible ways to handle the "What if?" I don't know how I drove to work the next day with a pounding headache coming from feeling worried and scared. My automatic pilot must have taken over.

The construction workers and my boss were at the office when I arrived. They admitted knowing the trench was really deep and frightening. The workers had rigged a board, side to side, to allow anyone entering or exiting the building to walk the plank. Yes, I walked the plank to get into the building. All day long, the thoughts of the scary plank walk caused me to fuss and fret. For many weeks and months, I found it difficult to let go of the fear of what could have happened. This created a definite change in my attitude toward fears. No longer could I brush off my fears. My safety is serious business, something no longer to be taken for granted. I had taken a big step into full time aging.

And yet, another fear of falling situation came along. This time, I was a silver sage. I tripped over a crack in an uneven sidewalk, then fell down onto the cement walkway. Even though the business complex had been built about twenty-five years earlier, it appeared to be well maintained. As I was falling, I remember thinking, "This can't be happening to me. What is happening?" Then my body turned slightly, which caused me to fall onto my left side, pinning my left arm under me.

The car keys flew from my hand, as my purse slipped off my right arm. When I tried to grab the purse, my right foot twisted, cushioning the purse and its contents as they spilled over my foot.

I knew I had fallen on the cement sidewalk, but the rest of the fall was a blur. A man came out of his office to ask how I felt. He explained he saw me trip and fall. There was a natural separation from one block of cement to the next that had aged unevenly during the years. Even sidewalks get older!

We assessed the results of my fall, noting the broken key chain, the splattered contents of my purse, ripped slacks, and so on. He would not let me even try to stand up.

The best thing he did was to assure me how important it was to stay right there and rest, while he talked with me. The fear and confusion made me want to get out of there as fast as possible.

However, the man's soothing voice enabled me to do the wise thing by following his instructions to calm down. I accepted his strength then, along with help from his adult son, I stood, took a few steps, rested, then walked to my appointment.

This accident caused so many fears to come to the fore that would not have entered my mind when I was younger: What if I'm disabled, left alone to face years of suffering? What if my money won't last as long as expected due to health care bills an accident might generate? Will I be too frail and weak to take care of myself? Will I be left alone to die with memory lapses? That's what fear does to seniors. It leads to obsessing about What if . . . what if . . .

The day after the trip and fall accident, the doctor, along with the physical therapist, worked with me on daily exercises to help facilitate the healing processes. I gladly accepted their guidance and suggestions. For six weeks, I wore a brace on my left arm, along with icing my foot and leg. Now I do stair stepping exercises to keep my legs and feet flexible to improve my balance on a daily basis.

Life goes on! Let's make the most of it.

To satisfy my mind, I went back to the office complex to check on the condition of the sidewalk. Fortunately, the two men who had come to my rescue happened to be walking out of their office, while I cautiously walked to the scene. I thanked them repeatedly for being so supportive, calming, and caring. After my fall, they decided to check the sidewalk, as well as having a talk with the building management. The crack was just the separation between two slabs of cement, which had shifted a bit over the years. Nothing could be done to fix it. Finding closure is important. Being aware, in order to accept the process of aging as the cause of a slight loss of physical balance, is essential.

The physical part of aging is a real problem, especially for many vain women. I ask myself what if I stay fat and wrinkled, never losing the turkey gobbler neck, losing my balance, and on and on. There are creams, lotions, and pills to slow our skin's aging, enabling us to look younger. These products are marketed to seniors who want their early stages of life to return and think they can be youthful again. Get real! It's impossible to wipe off or exercise away a turkey gobbler neck that has been there for twenty years.

These products give hope, and some do help temporarily, but no magic cure is available. If these products work today, they will stop working when you stop using them. It becomes a lifetime commitment to the product. We all want hope, but false hope makes reality much worse. It is time to accept me for the real me. What if these products and procedures take my time and money then leave me worse than the original me?

I want to look like the real me, not a pasted, painted, implanted, carved out woman. What if it was acceptable and admirable for each of us to be true to ourselves? I certainly don't want to fake it until I make it to the end, without ever being the real me. What a waste of a wonderful person!

From time to time, I wonder if it is important to listen to the little voice in my head warning me, or if I am experiencing the "What if's" of aging. What if the edginess I felt while driving home led me to take a wrong turn, which acted as protection from an accident that occurred along the original route? Or did I forget to make the correct turn at the right place because I was not concentrating? Life presents difficult challenges.

What if . . . we are programmed to age?

What if . . . we could change that program?

12

Disposable Society

We live in a disposable society. How and when did that happen? Technically, it's called planned obsolescence. Manufacturers create plastic bags, one time use cameras, disposable razors, throw away plastic water bottles, and so much more to help busy consumers. Who cares enough to think about the long term consequences? How can we teach kids to respect their belongings when objects aren't made to last a long time?

Manufacturers don't guarantee their products as they did during the last century. Auto companies don't warranty their cars when the reasonable time comes for breakdowns. Get a new one instead of fixing it! Today's generation does not understand how we respected and cared for the goods we bought with hard earned salaries. Maybe I am out of step with our disposable society by continuing to expect value from my purchases.

The printer head in my computer printer would not move back and forth. I bought it three years earlier, expecting it to last as long as the computer would last. The cost was only slightly lower to fix it than to replace the whole thing. Of course, I bought a new one, which caused me to have to learn a completely new set of installation and use directions. I tried to donate the old printer, but no one wanted a fixer-upper. Computers and ancillary products quickly become obsolete, so they are disposable. I question why we need to buy warranties if the product is disposable? What a waste of resources to clutter the environment.

Cell phones are updated every year. When the one to two year contract is over, it is almost necessary to get a new phone to keep up with the technology. The idea of respecting a phone by taking care of it is almost nonexistent. After all, we will get a new one soon!

Does this phenomenon apply only to technology? Definitely not! You can see it in the business world. When an owner wants to save money, he or she downsizes older employees, reorganizes, and hires younger people at lower salaries. Everyone can be replaced, especially in the business world.

In restaurants, when it's time to raise prices, owners create new and improved menus, showing flashy pictures of new items. Are we fooled? Not silver sages! We are aware consumers.

Clothing is another example to question our disposable society. Styles change, causing us to throw out old clothes to make space for today's trends. Fortunately, some people donate clothing to help others in need. There are many collection centers, such as the American Cancer Society, who will pick up from your home or office.

Clothing does not have to be disposable if it's out of style with today's ideas. Young people criticize seniors for wearing the same clothes over and over, especially when they are judged to be out of style. I have two sets of clothes, one for around the house and one to wear in public. The nicer outfits do not get much use, so I wear them often but for a short time. I feel comfortable in my familiar outfits, so I'll keep and wear them for a long time. I don't care about current fad fashions. They aren't suitable for my stage of life.

Are any disposables helpful and wonderful? Most of them are useful and handy. Consider disposable diapers, baby wipes, toilet paper, napkins, ballpoint pens, doctors' rubber gloves, cotton balls, plastic silverware, paper cups, paper plates, toothbrushes, razor blades, and zillions of other things invented to make our lives easier. Many of them are destroying the environment. Is that really disposable?

What is not disposable?

Friendships. Sometimes they fizzle out due to life changes that alter a friendship from what it used to be into something less desirable. True friendship is so rare, it is difficult to envision letting it go.

Jan and I met at a class attended by people of all ages and all stages of life. Our lives and backgrounds were so different. It was hard to imagine then accept how we became friends, creative business partners, and best friends. We cried and clung onto each other when she moved to Missouri. The friendship became less convenient, causing us to wean ourselves from frequent contacts. But the uniqueness of this friendship meant it never really ended. It was not disposable. Jan died about six years ago. I can still hear her cigarette coughs or her voice talking to me, or see her driving down the street. Jan and I had a true friendship. Love is a feeling. It is not disposable.

Is income disposable? Financial analysts will ask about your "disposable" income. It is not designed to be thrown away after use. They are asking how much of your income can you live without, after all the bills and taxes are paid?

Because money changes hands so quickly, it gives the appearance of being disposable. Bills and coins can be recycled, but the true exchange value varies. We must keep finding new sources to earn money to excel in our materialistic world.

Ah, the good old days of bartering! My friend is a twin, who decided to write a book about twins in order to share their experiences. I proofread her chapters every week in exchange for her husband cutting my hair every month. What a great deal for both of us!

There are clubs around the country offering free membership for bartering of goods and others for bartering of time. This is the link for time bartering:

http://www.timebanks.org/

People are not disposable. When a marriage does not work, get a divorce. Find a new state of the art mate. This advice means today's model will soon be obsolete. Good grief!

When Grandpa becomes senile, ship him out to a care facility until he dies. Living longer gives us a quantity of life but not necessarily a quality of life. People share love, they are not disposable!

Sometimes, people are like garbage trucks. They run around filled with life's garbage, full of frustration, full of anger, and full of disappointment. As their garbage piles up, they need a place to dump it. Occasionally they will dump it on you. Of course, we are led to believe, it's nothing personal! Never take garbage and spread it to other people at work, at home, or on the streets. Waste garbage is disposable; however, no person to person dumping is allowed! Don't give it out and don't accept it from others.

Our planet is in trouble with all the garbage we produce. Is garbage permanently disposable? Much more research is required to solve this serious problem.

Is religion disposable? If the value is gone, then it can be considered a throwaway. How does that apply to religion? When I was young, I thought God was like Superman, flying around in the sky with a powerful cape. People would look up when they prayed, so I assumed he must be up there, strong, powerful, and available. I never questioned the teachings or the gender of God.

My parents arranged for me to attend Sunday school with religious services, especially during the sacred holidays. Everything said and done was an ancient ritual with an honorable history of tradition.

Since the religious services were not in English, I didn't want to attend, but I did so because my parents wanted the three of us to go together. Love is not disposable, but habits can be changed.

I believed in and accepted my family's religion, but something wasn't right. When someone dies, the prayer we say includes a phrase thanking God for taking our loved one. Mom suffered so much with cancer. Why didn't God take her before all the suffering? This questioning was a defining time in my thinking. It made me certain I had become an atheist.

After moving to California, I attended services of many different faiths searching to find the most comfortable place. The modern psychological and philosophical approach from metaphysics, which examines the nature of reality, became my spiritual path. I did not dispose of my religion. Instead, I added this new dimension to look further into the unknown for the balanced meaning of life.

Having faith does not mean you don't have doubts. Questioning is very good. In fact, it is necessary in order to grow and develop in a positive direction. I believe faith is not disposable. Formal religion? Well, you decide for yourself.

13

Don't Worry, Be Happy!

Happiness is a method of traveling rather than a destination. Take it slow and easy to check out many of the wandering roads to find happiness.

There are many stages of happiness, depending on our current phase of life. I giggled with delight as Daddy threw me into the air when I was a baby. My parents bought me a record player with forty-five rpm records for my thirteenth birthday. I was so excited about getting the gift I really, really wanted. I felt overwhelmed by their thoughtfulness. I couldn't stop jumping around with excitement. Records played in the house and enjoyed by the whole family for many years.

When my prom date brought a corsage of yellow sunflowers with large green leaves, disappointment showed in my face and expressive eyes. Oh, good grief, how could I wear that thing and deal with my peers making fun of me?

As we were walking out the door, my boyfriend turned around to walk back to the kitchen. He came out with a broad bright smile, and I a huge wrist corsage of twelve perfect yellow roses to match my pale yellow dress. I was so thrilled with his creativity and caring that I laughed and smiled until I couldn't breathe from the happiness and from feeling special. After learning to breathe again, we went to a wonderful high school prom. No other girl in the room had such a huge, gorgeous wrist corsage floral arrangement. I felt special and loved!

Happiness is a joy of various intensities. It swells up from inside and breaks out in the form of smiles, squealing, yelling, giggling, and even throwing up. Yes, I had a friend who threw up when her boyfriend proposed. They have been married for twenty-five years! Happiness is a cheerful, challenging path that can lead to a wonderful emotional experience.

Happiness is on the path to learning more about technology, current events, writing, and psychology. It is seeing and hearing how others are enjoying this moment in time. I choose to be happy now. I know when I feel a happy glow, even if others don't see it in my smiling face. Sometimes it's an inside job!

Memories of happiness never end, especially when they help to increase self-esteem. Keep in mind how those memories felt? How did your body react? What were you thinking? Write it down to experience them again.

Mature happiness is more of a knowing that old stressors don't have to exist anymore. It is no longer a matter of accepting a grueling pace to succeed at work, yet telling everyone how great it is to do the job. Happiness is more like a quiet choice to see the good in today and in every moment.

For me, happiness is choosing to wear lavender since it has always been my favorite color, not because it is in favor this season. Happiness is a feeling of acceptance while I enjoy the laughter and noises of the children walking to school every morning. Their cheerfulness is contagious.

If an encore career is in your vision, choose work more like a hobby than a job. At least think of it as a hobby, concentrating on the pleasure it brings to your life. Satisfaction comes when the daily pressure is lifted. Being active and fulfilled daily is a dream come true.

In years gone by, a senior was a retired person or one who reached age sixty-five. Retirement rules have changed, and so has our perception of who is a senior. There are so many rough times during the aging process. Each of us has to face them in our own way.

I'm unique! So lose the titles identifying seniors, such as "youngster" or "madam." Either just talk or ask for my name, then use it. I'm Marcia. Hearing my name gives me a familiar feeling, a special happy glow. I sure wish I had a sense of humor about those cutesy names. Don't worry. Be happy!

It's important to act silly by making goofy faces, laughing out loud, jumping with enthusiasm at a sports game, kicking autumn leaves, splashing in the rain, applying the gift of optimism to current events, and giving yourself a big, warm hug. Doing these things with someone else spreads the delight even further.

New events can be the path to happiness. As Aunt Edith always told us, when one door closes, another one opens. Often, when we look at a closed door for so long we aren't able to see the new door open and waiting for us. It's never too late to begin again.

When my parents bought a house, we moved about a forty-minute drive from our previous little house. For years and years, I wrote school assignments about how unfair my parents were to take me away from my friends, when I was age twelve. Life definitely changed when I eventually did make new friends. In reality, I did like the newer, bigger house, which was closer to our family. Once I stopped staring at the closed door and opened the door to my new life, my joy blossomed.

Happiness is everywhere for us to enjoy as long as we concentrate on seeing and feeling the delight. Feeling good is such a great place to be. It is worth the challenges! Giving is the best, loving pleasure. Happiness never ends.

I enjoy seeing and hearing Sammy, our cat, in high spirits. Sometimes I take a can of tuna, with the can opener, over to the kitchen counter, knowing he will appear in the room immediately. Sammy meows and meows to make sure I know he is there, ready and waiting to share my lunch. His meows, along with watching him enjoy the tuna, mean happiness for both of us at the same time. The process causes me to go into a high pitched baby talk while having a one way conversation with the cat. The conversation is cheerful, silly and loving.

Happiness is contagious. Spread it around! Cheerfulness builds relationships, especially when coupled with laughter.

After Mom had her kidney removed, the world seemed to come to a stop when we were told it was cancer. It worried me thinking someone might go into her hospital room with a cloud of gloom and doom hovering over them. In those days, doctors did not believe in telling patients the bad news for fear the patients would become depressed and not try to live. So, we pretended that everything was okay.

I dwelled on the idea of bringing laughter into Mom's room and into her life. I remembered the story about Norman Cousin's proven success with laughter therapy. He was a writer who worked in the medical field and had many

121

other successes. He developed a recovery program incorporating a positive attitude, love, faith, hope, and laughter. Cousin's mission in life was to give healing peace. He discovered ten minutes of genuine belly laughter from watching Marx Brothers' films had the anesthetic effect of giving patients two hours of pain free sleep.

When the effects wore off, they would watch another ten minutes of the movie. The key is to promote happiness with good health and laughter.

My creativity came to the fore when I decided to send a special bouquet of flowers to the hospital for Mom. Two florists would not fill my order, saying mom's surgery was too serious for such a silly gift. With great determination, and knowing I was right and they were wrong, I pushed forward until I found a florist who would honor my request. The next day, the florist delivered a silver metal hospital bedpan filled with a variety of bright colored flowers!

Mom loved the unusual, silly, creative idea. It encouraged her to laugh several times a day when she was alone and when someone came into her room. She would point out the flower arrangement to visitors so they could share in the laughter.

Be happy! Laughter is the best medicine!

The award winning song, "Don't Worry, Be Happy" has a far-reaching message, telling us to expect some trouble in our lives, however when you worry, trouble will double. Keep the problems in perspective by planning for happiness. Avoid worrying. It can create illnesses from the stress. Worrying does not solve problems, actions do.

Happiness principles:

1. Feel happy! Laughter is the best medicine.
2. Inner happiness can't be taken away.
3. Fill your day with activities that make your heart glow.
4. Give a compliment every day.
5. Smile at yourself in the mirror and give yourself a hug.
6. Forgive and let go. Do not hold a grudge.
7. Appreciate what you do have.

Laughter is like taking a mini vacation. Social interaction stimulates your brain to release *feel good* chemicals like *nor epinephrine*, which leads to contentment. Spend time with compatible friends to discuss what makes each one feel happy.

Mature happiness is a knowing the old stressors don't have to exist anymore. It's no longer necessary to accept a grueling pace to succeed at work competition. It's more like a quiet choice to see the good in today and in every moment. Happiness can be found when the daily pressure is lifted. Don't worry, be happy!

Happiness is eating dessert before dinner, acting on an impulse to e-mail old family photos to my cousins, and even buying myself an easy to use knife sharpener.

Gratitude increases satisfaction with life. Express gratitude to everyone you appreciate, especially during times of kindness from others.

Happiness is amplified by talking and writing about it, especially savoring the small pleasures. Sometimes it's an inside job! When was the last time your thanked yourself for being a giving person?

The happiest people spend the least time alone. Not all activities have to be pre-planned and pre-organized. People watching is such a fascinating sport. Go to the local mall, sit down on a bench, then watch the people walking, talking, and window shopping. It's okay to be critical of the mid-lifer who is wearing a too short mini skirt as long as you don't say anything out loud. Find the cutest haircut on a female and on a male. Oh, so many things to observe while people watching. No worries, no cares, just watching and smiling.

When I was unexpectedly downsized out of my last job, I was not prepared to move on with a new life. Trumpeting shock took over at first. Then writing gave me the unanticipated opportunity to see life from a different point of view. Once I stopped staring at the closed door, in favor of opening up the door to my new life, my happiness increased.

Giving is the best loving cheerfulness that could ever exist. Happiness never ends. Small forms of giving are much appreciated and easy to provide. A smile for someone who opens the door, "thank you" for the person who picked up your dropped credit card, a show of appreciation with a tip for the plumber who never gets a tip, and giving home baked lasagna for the neighbor who said good-bye to her college bound son today.

Music lovers know the delight of listening to performers, of playing an instrument, and of singing in the shower. Be unique; enjoy your singing in the car, while cleaning the house, getting dressed and while cooking in the kitchen.

Do you worry about what others think about you? Will they like your new shoes, hairstyle, giggle laughter or your passion for apples cut into 8 slices? Those people are so busy thinking about themselves; they don't have the time or energy to think about you. Forget about them! Be accountable to yourself.

You are the only judge of yourself that matters. Honor your true self.

14

Life Is Like a Bowl of Cherries

**The older you get, the tougher it is to lose weight,
because by then your body and your fat
are really good friends.**

Dieting is my Achilles' heel; it's my weakness in spite of my overall strength. The idea of dieting is to lose weight, which means I'll find it again. That's been my lifelong routine of losing and finding. Die is the root word of dieting. How horrible!

During a few fleeting years here and there, I was "lookin' good," wearing a so called average dress size, feeling fine, and within the normal to high range of the charts in the doctor's office.

How many times did I hear adults tell me, "Being a model is perfect for a tall girl like you." Wow! I was in the Sears Chubby Club fashion shows! I hated showing my overweight body to the world. But it might lead to modeling work. Sure! Right!

By age twelve I had slimmed down, transforming eating habits to control my weight. Feeling stressed has always caused me to turn the word stressed around to read it backwards, to give me an excuse to eat desserts. Desserts spelled backwards equals stressed!

While I took care of Mom when she was sick and dying, I turned to smoking instead of eating. The day she died from lung cancer, the cigarettes went into the trash with a powerful pitch of both arms. Losing thirty five pounds and looking thin did not make me beautiful. My collarbones and rib bones were protruding. At five feet, nine inches, I wore a size fourteen dress. The stress, coupled with not eating, caused me to look too skinny to be healthy. I still didn't wear anything near model size clothing. So much for relying on the bathroom scale numbers!

The reason for a larger than expected dress size was "you have big bones!" Life can be exhausting and frustrating!

Current research results explain there are psychological reasons plus family genetics for weight issues. It can't be blamed just on overeating, although it is the obvious problem.

Can you relate to my lifelong struggle with being overweight? We live in a society which values readily available delicious foods, but criticizes those who are obese. If I wanted to be fat, I would not complain about this dis-ease (dis-comfort). Aging as an overweight person is a complicated, uncomfortable way to live.

Most overweight people want to be healthier and look more presentable. Here I am, embarrassed by the major hardship of being obese, yet bravely revealing the trauma to help you and to help me. That should earn me some brownie points!

Obesity leads to more problems than anyone can imagine, such as sleep apnea. When sleep is constantly interrupted by snoring and other breathing problems, the body craves carbohydrates, which leads to weight gain. Being overweight is extremely difficult. Serious medical and emotional problems can cause additional problems with age. It is not a choice, it is a curse! It's the pits!

When I was teaching, the reduction in classroom funding created a decision to eliminate physical education programs in the elementary schools. The teachers knew obesity would be a problem in the not too distant future. Medical professionals strongly advocated exercise in the form of school physical education. Now more specialists realize we were correct in our assessment. Additional educational money cuts are always being threatened, without a realistic view of the effect on our children. The bowl of being in the pits is filling up!

Meeting new friends is "the pits," to use that phrase again from my teen years. After weeks of attending classes in a new junior high, I did not meet anyone who would talk with me, who could become my friend. Whenever I would gather the confidence to start a conversation, it seems classmates ignored me. I didn't know how to interact with strangers who were my peers. As an only child, I was used to being with familiar friends or adults.

Mom told me to compliment them on something I really did like. No false compliments! She called this "killing them with kindness." After a few days of doing this and nothing changing, Mom continued to tell me to speak up, make eye contact, and be complimentary. In due time, it did work. I made a few friends, eventually joined a high school sorority, and I didn't feel the sad isolation anymore. Problems are opportunities to learn for today and for the future!

These experiences reminded me how the same is true for me today. Making new friends isn't any easier for me today than it was when I was in high school. I continue to do the best I can, going outside my comfort zone. The more things change, the more they stay the same. Mom's advice applies to the challenges of meeting friends today.

The humorist Erma Bombeck said it best:
> **Life is like a bowl of cherries, mostly sweet**
> **with a few pits. Why am I in the pits?**

Let's Play 20 Questions

The path to a more successful life is to get to know yourself better. Ask questions, pay attention to your answers. Take stock of yourself, often!

My favorite color is:

I like the movie:

The best thing about me is:

My favorite word is:

The best gift I ever received was:

My favorite sound is:

The best show on television is:

because I like:

My dream is to:

I like to talk about:

I wish:

My favorite song is:

because:

I would like to be age:

so that I could:

I'm afraid of:

I'd like to go to:

I believe in miracles because:

The silliest, most goofy thing I ever did was:

I love:

I feel happy when:

I'm most proud of myself for:

My best quality is:

Now you can answer the question---"Who Am I?"
I am:

Part Four: *Family*

15

Thanks, Mom

What were the first things Mom taught me? She taught me patience and forgiveness by example, right from my birth.

Mom was in labor seventy-two hours because I was not ready to be born. I turned sideways! The doctor said it was going to be a long wait. There wasn't anything to do until I decided to turn around. The doctor went to the hospital in his party tuxedo to hold Mom's hands several times during the wait. He would leave for a while to celebrate New Year's Eve at parties, then return hours later to check on us. I was born a healthy baby girl at 9:35 p.m. on New Year's Day. Everyone involved learned patience!

Mom taught me how to tie my shoes, keep my room clean, speak to my elders with respect, balance a checkbook, and everyday good manners. The usual loving, caring, patient mom stuff!

I listened to Mom's words of wisdom along with her special sayings, while wondering if she really thought I understood what she was saying when I nodded, agreed, and smiled. Well, those conversations must have worked to teach me more things than I could have ever imagined during my childhood. Not only did I repeat her words when a situation was ripe for wisdom, but I was also repeating the wisdom handed down from her parents, too.

My son Hal, also did a lot of listening, nodding, smiling, and repeating whenever I took up the chants from those two generations, added my own, and passed them on to him. As an adult, he has kept up the family tradition by passing on the insights. He has some friends who use those expressions, in addition to spreading them to a new generation. I don't think they can realize how exciting it is to know how they show loving gratitude and respect by passing on the wisdom of silver sages.

I've learned the meaning of some of those family expressions from living my life. Mom used to say, "You can get used to hanging if you hang long enough." Huh? Who hangs? Why would I hang?

My son would not believe he was intelligent. He frequently found ways to prove he was right and I was wrong. After his twenty-eighth birthday, I started to see a change in his conversations and interests. Aha! Maturity! I had been hanging and waiting for all those years, getting used to his lack of confidence as well as his childish attitude. I finally hung on so long that I got used to hanging! Mom was right, be patient. Good news—I'm not hanging anymore!

One spring day, I came home from elementary school and walked into the kitchen with muddy shoes while Mom was on her hands and knees, scrubbing the floor. It was the only time she ever gave me a spanking! What happened to her patience? I thought she probably wanted to leave me outside to be raised by aliens! Mom let me know how displeased she was with my lack of respect for her hard cleaning work.

Later in the evening, we ended up hugging each other while crying, which led to smiles and giggles. We forgave each other! Both of us realized just how tired and stressed Mom was and how I was being a typical, unaware, careless kid.

I have often wondered about people who came into my life with behavior that was out of sync with the situation. I felt hurt, knowing I did not deserve to receive their powerful negativity. Why were they shouting in anger or showing disapproval? Were they extremely stressed out, or was it really me being inappropriate? Surface behaviors do not always reflect one's inner feelings. Mom would tell me either to be patient with them by giving them kindness, or get away from them so they can deal with their own problems. The fight or flight response was a useful learning tool.

Mom and I talked a lot with each other, discussing my particular problems as well as life in general. Those were the times when I learned the most from her without realizing how these were life's serious lessons.

Mom always wanted to be like Amelia Earhart, flying across the Atlantic, winning awards, attempting to break more pilot flying records, and being a famous Aviatrix. For decades, I wanted to take flying lessons. It all sounded so exciting. Finally, when I didn't make it happen, I realized how being an Aviatrix was Mom's dream, not mine. We were so close with caring and sharing. Sometimes, I took on her interests as if they were my own.

Our neighbors said they would see one of us on the front porch and frequently not know whether it was Mom or me sitting on the glider. We did look alike and dress alike. Mom was one of the first women of that generation to stop wearing housedresses. We both wore blue jeans and long shirts. Neither of us had sisters, so we shared a rewarding and unique togetherness, yet we honored our special roles as mom and daughter.

Dad, Mom, and I cooperated as a family unit when cleaning up after meals. At the end of dinner, Dad and I cleared the table, Mom washed the dishes, then I dried and placed them back into the cupboards. These were terrific times, working together in the kitchen while sharing feelings. Sometimes we made up silly poems or sang "The

Name Game" (also known as "The Banana Song") or tried to talk like well known movie actors. We often laughed our way through the kitchen work.

Each of our bedrooms had a tiny closet crammed full of clothes. Dad bought a small metal closet for his clothes in the spare bedroom. Our winter clothes were stored in boxes in the attic, which were taken down at the first signs of winter. Then the boxes were filled with the light weight clothes for the warmer weather and stored back up in the attic. What a biannual project we endured!

We still had the annoying problem of two women, with their many blouses of various sleeve lengths and fabrics, not being able to hang up their clothes in the small closets. Dad attached a strong clothesline in two places in the basement to enable us to hang blouses so they wouldn't get squashed or wrinkled.

In those days, everything had to be ironed, including bed sheets and even handkerchiefs! Mom and I shared the blouses, since we wore the same size. Whoever got up first, picked first—unless I really, really wanted a particular blouse to wear the next day, then I would pick it the night before. Mom said I was to pick first. Me first! We didn't always have the same taste, so some of the blouses were never shared. The chance to not share was nice too.

We never really discussed "woman's work," but the routine of the times was for the woman to do the housework and the man to earn a living. In our family, Mom and Dad both worked in their clothing store, which enabled them to hire someone to clean house and do laundry. When my parents sold the store, everything changed at home. Mom worked all week, and I attended high school. We cleaned and did laundry on Saturday, while Dad worked as an electrician six days a week. Hiring someone to help in the house was not financially possible.

Every Saturday, Mom and I argued all day. I resented having to do housework, and without my knowing it, so did Mom. Still, the cleaning and laundry had to be done. At the end of the day, Dad would come home, carefully open the door, and ask if it was safe for him to come in. Were we in the middle of a verbal battle? That was his real question. Sometimes I would be boiling with anger over the unfairness of having to spend my whole Saturday, every Saturday, helping with housework. I didn't want Dad or anyone else to try to calm me down. It wasn't fair!

After the anger and the resentment built up through the months, Mom and I finally talked about it and came to an understanding. We had to get through this rough patch. Things will get better. The best is yet to come. Thanks, Mom. I used the same approach many times in my life, taking one day at a time. One of my favorite expressions is "Just do it." Don't get emotionally involved or procrastinate, just get it done. Perhaps this extremely difficult time was when I also learned to take the most unpleasant aspect of any job and do it first. Get the worst part out of the way first.

Many people don't have good relationships with their moms. Through the years, I've heard many complaints about neither side being willing to talk a problem out in order to arrive at a truce. No one person was completely at fault in the relationship. The blame game raged on and on. The anger festered, causing havoc with other relationships.

**People unable to make peace with their past,
just screw up their present!**

I can't imagine not having a loving, caring relationship and friendship with my mom. Thanks, Mom.

Turn the word MOM upside down and you'll get WOW. My Mom was a WOW!

16

Daddy's Little Girl

So many questions, so little time! Dad was patient, calm, and reserved. He talked while bragging about his work after becoming an electrical contractor, especially when he had a captive audience. He wasn't a man to engage in small talk. During my childhood, we were comfortable talking with each other.

Even before attending elementary school, I always asked one after the other "why" questions. Dad was patient, trying to answer as much as he could, but when the questions became too complicated, he learned to tell the truth. He didn't know the answer.

My family often commented on the unusual detailed questions I asked, especially for such a young child. The questions started with the word "why." My questions start the same way today! "Why is the sky blue?" and "Why is up called up?" They weren't the usual repetitive "why" questions most children ask. Family said there were more complex inquiries than they could answer, along with many follow-up questions.

Why are some people left handed while others are right handed? Dad was born a lefty; however, the teachers forced him to learn to be a righty to conform to the standards of the times. Among other things, he learned to use regular scissors and to write with his right hand. As time went on, he followed the rules by continuing to lead with his right hand, but always preferred to use his dominant left hand.

Dad taught himself to be ambidextrous. He could write with both hands at the same time! It was exciting to see him show off for my friends and me. He had a personal explanation for my "why" question about having a dominant hand. The stories encouraged me to remember to use both hands instead of expecting my right hand to do all the work. I liked personal answers the best. They gave me the opportunity to learn more about my dad.

I still ask "Why?" When doctors try to shuffle me out of the office too fast, I've learned to sit still long enough to ask questions, unless my brain goes "out to lunch" from the stress. Several bosses showed anger when I asked those detailed "why" questions. I needed to understand the fine points before I could work on projects. Their anger usually meant they didn't know the answer but were too ego driven to admit it. Dad told me he welcomed questions from me, but I wasn't to expect strangers to be so responsive to my questioning. Wow! Dad was right on!

One day, Mom was upset with me. She told Dad the story. It happened so long ago I don't remember exactly what happened to cause so much distress. Dad sat me down on his lap, calmly explaining why I was wrong, then advised me on the correct way to handle the problem. I felt so miserable and crushed over upsetting my parents that I cried and cried! It was obvious I was wrong and I knew it, but he was being so nice to explain it to me in a loving manner. To this day, I get emotional when anyone expresses loving support with patience. Mistakes do happen. I'd like to be perfect, but I can face the reality of knowing perfection is never going to happen!

Dad frequently reinforced one of his favorite sayings during good times: "Appreciate the ups, because the downs seem to last longer." It's the truth! He also liked to say, "This too shall pass." There are cycles to life, change is necessary. Patiently take one step at a time, then remember to temper the negative with the knowledge that this too shall pass. Then fully appreciate the ups. Carpe Diem—seize the day!

There was a time during my teen years when I was freaking out, worried about being an old maid, a spinster living alone. Dad didn't know how to handle these girly things, but he did tell me to appreciate this down time, while it's quiet, because soon I'll be busier with dates than I ever expected.

About a month later, I started dating a cute guy on Fridays and an intelligent college student on Saturdays. Then, when I received a call from a third guy, I realized Dad was right about the down times getting all mixed with the up periods. A teen can never have too many dates, although it can become complicated.

The interview panel at the Pittsburgh Public Schools asked me if I knew how to play the piano, a requirement for teaching kindergarten. Student teaching had reinforced my passion for teaching kindergarten children. I said yes, then went home to tell my parents I had to buy a piano so I could learn to play. What bravery for reserved, quiet me! Showing self-confidence in the interview had worked. They hired me as a kindergarten teacher, which gave me the opportunity take piano lessons for a couple of years on a used piano, while saving up to buy a beautiful new upright piano.

I progressed from playing scales, to starter songs, to kindergarten songs, to playing some real adult songs. That is when I bought the sheet music for "Daddy's Little Girl" and practiced it every day. Yes, every day!

Mom would watch TV upstairs in her room with the door closed. With his usual, great patience, Dad would listen to my practice sessions without complaining. The piano was in the dining room, next to the kitchen where he read the newspaper every evening. He received the full blast of all those piano playing mistakes, but he never said a word, except to mention periodically how he noticed I was improving.

During my wedding reception, I instructed the band to play "Daddy's Little Girl" three times. Dad and I danced each time. During each dance, he reminded me how I used to dance with him by stepping on his feet while he did the footwork for both of us. Whenever we attended family celebrations, like weddings or anniversary parties, everyone knew that Daddy and his little girl would be dancing.

Dad was very handy, able to fix broken toys as well as complete most fix-it projects around the house. I really enjoyed watching him work on projects while learning from his demonstrations. I used to tell people how my daddy could fix anything!

Dad would wake up at four in the morning in the winter, to shovel coal into the furnace so the house would be comfortable and warm for Mom and me. He was the go-to man for fixing things.

I vividly remember the spring day when a heavy rainstorm caused our basement to flood. Dad would not let Mom or me go into the water to retrieve things from down there. For a short time, I sat on an upper step, which led from the kitchen to the basement. We talked as he pulled photographs and other things out of the cold, dirty water, in order to salvage whatever could be saved.

At one point, he was breathing hard, then stood straight, and stretched. He told me to go upstairs and close the kitchen door behind me. He was going to open the basement window to let the smells out of the room. Dad was having a difficult time breathing in the debris and stagnant water. He did not want the smells to make us sick. I knew I definitely wanted those considerate characteristics in my husband, someday!

If Dad had a computer, he would have found answers to my questions, or still better, "we" would have gone to the computer to find out "why?"

To a father growing old, nothing is dearer than a daughter. -- Euripides

17

Sibling Love, Sibling Rivalry

How did my birth order in the family affect my life? The only child is unique as the first and last born children in their families. By spending so much time with adults, they are treated like responsible and capable "little adults."

I am an only child who married an only child and had an only child. No siblings, no sibling rivalry, no sibling love!

The only child is often asked, "Don't you miss not having sisters or brothers?" Speculating about something I've never experienced is odd. Through the years, I have changed my answer according to the current phase of my life. Usually I was self reliant and fine. At other times, I missed not having a support system, which I thought might be attained by a cherished sibling or two.

As a child, I took full responsibility for everything I did. No siblings, no shifting blame to anyone else. By the same token, I never had to fight blame given to me by a sibling. Monetary gifts were not given to spoil me, but I was spoiled by not having to share attention or love. I learned how to entertain myself during my childhood, so I did not miss having playmate siblings.

Despite the stereotype of an only child unable to adjust to the so-called normal world, we are some of the most well adjusted people on earth. Our maturity and intelligence levels tend to be higher than those of children from large families.

When I was twelve, we moved to a neighborhood with a new, large, combined junior/senior high school. A girl down the street, a year ahead of me, agreed to walk with me to school and back home on a daily basis. I was grateful, knowing I didn't have to walk the long distance alone, especially on the first day. Walking to school for forty-five minutes, seeing the sights, and talking with her, could have been rewarding.

Unfortunately, she never met me after school the first day, leaving me to walk home alone. Good thing I paid attention during the morning walk, I was able to find my way back home. But the disappointment crushed my ego. Later in the evening, she apologized for having to stay after school and not being able to get a message to me. It was obvious, she did not want me tagging along. But, the first day trauma of walking to school was over. From that point on, I walked to and from school alone. An only child quickly learns self-sufficiency. Maybe siblings, who were a little older, would have come in handy. Younger ones? Not so much!

Many only children succeed in careers requiring independence, ability to concentrate, decisiveness, and personal accountability. A sense of responsibility above and beyond the call of duty can be vital and appreciated. Women who exhibit such traits can be resented by coworkers as well as bosses, for being so capable. Men with those traits are rewarded and promoted. It's still an old fashioned imbalance in life, which we hope is changing.

After trying for many years "to hide my light under a bushel" by being quiet and just doing my job, I realized how often I was helping others while harming myself. It's tough to find the light, let alone stay in it, without support. Some siblings do not support each other, so that leaves me wondering whether siblings would have really made any difference. It's probably a matter of individual differences.

I don't think having a sibling would have made any difference in problem situations at work, except to teach me how to handle confrontations. The same problems occur when I have to deal with customer service representatives. I never had practice with siblings to learn to argue or negotiate for success.

Maybe, if I had siblings, I would have been more involved in group events with a variety of people. I could have developed communication skills by interacting with others. The practice would have taught me how to negotiate and fight for myself, while generally being more confident and assertive.

Perhaps I would have grown up feeling sociable, instead of shy. Perhaps, possibly, maybe!

An only child can spend a lifetime being and feeling alone. Some say they never felt a void. I enjoy the natural healing powers of being alone, but not all the time. The quiet, calm, and uncomplicated environment is very rewarding. It is not enjoyable to always be alone, especially without at least co-workers to fill the social void. The adjustment for the aging, only child can be perplexing.

The most alone I ever felt was when I was married for the second time. We were not a "we." Instead, we functioned independently, continued to make our own decisions, and kept to ourselves. That's how I, as the only child, functioned with an only child spouse. I wanted us to be a sociable couple. My husband never learned and wasn't willing to learn how we could interact with each other in order to be a "we" and be sociable.

I think the differences in the silver sage years between having siblings and being the only child exist to varying degrees depending on whether the only child is in a relationship, has children in his or her primary family, or is living alone. Having other people in my daily life makes a huge difference in my positive outlook. Few things can compare to a good laugh. If you want to give an only child a much appreciated present, give the gift of laughter. TV is my home laughter machine!

Writing has prompted me to look back many years to review my unique life as an only child. Perhaps I would have been less lonely if I had siblings, especially during times of family strife. Friends have said I'm lucky, I don't have to deal with wild and outrageous sibling rivalry. I never had the feeling Mom loved someone else more! Individual experiences and perspectives are important considerations. I play the cards of life that are dealt to me.

Being an only child is not a perfect hand, but what is flawless and ideal?

The only child as President of the USA.

Only four U.S. presidents out of forty-four can be considered only children:

The following four had half siblings:
Franklin D. Roosevelt
Gerald Ford
Bill Clinton
Barack Obama
Roosevelt had a younger half brother.
Ford had four half brothers and two half sisters.
Clinton has one younger half brother.

Obama has a half sister from his mother, and a half sister and a half brother from his father

18

My Two Bubbies

What's a Bubbie? My family called our grandmas by the traditional title of Bubbie. Since we saw my two bubbies frequently, they both had strong influences on my childhood. I wanted to easily distinguish which bubbie we were talking about, so I gave them special names. Their height difference must have had a big influence on me because I used it as the way to identify them.

I named my maternal grandmother Big Bubbie, because she was five feet six. I can clearly visualize Big Bubbie. Her salt and pepper hair was pulled back in a tight bun, the style of the times. I spent so much time at her home on weekends that I can still easily envision her printed housedresses and her full white apron with a bib top, always tied in the back.

I remember, she served family dinners at her house, Mom talked with her daily, and I stayed with her every weekend while my parents worked in their family business. Big Bubbie taught me how to play cards and how to measure with my hand instead of a measuring cup, among other skills. She taught me to appreciate nature's gifts of snowy winters, flowery summers, and autumn's gorgeous fall leaves. We took walks; kicked fall leaves while carefully listening to the crunch sounds, enjoyed the distinctive colors, appreciated the crisp air, and picked out patterns in the clouds. Today, I still enjoy fall as my favorite season of the year.

One weekend, when I was four years old, I played with the bathroom door lock. The long shiny key turned so easily that it fell on to the hallway wooden floor. I accidentally locked myself in the bathroom! The fire department came with truck sirens blaring. Big firefighters put up ladders, crawled through the window, then unlocked the door.

I was so embarrassed about doing such a ridiculous thing that caused so much commotion; I hid behind the flowing white window curtains or in the corner of the dining room. I was not willing to go out in the daylight because the neighbors might see me and make fun of me for causing so much trouble! It took a lot of Big Bubbie's tender loving care, in additional to loving talks to get me over the trauma! She was an accepting, loving woman.

After my tonsils were removed, when I was five, the family began noticing my weight gain. Big Bubbie knew how much I enjoyed eating baked potatoes with lots of sour cream. One evening, when I was about seven, she gave me something new on the market; she called it a non-fattening potato. Every weekend we ate our special secret treat. The smell was horrible and the taste seemed weird, but I was eating a non-fattening potato!

Not too long after Big Bubbie died, I asked Mom to buy the special potatoes like Big Bubbie had secretly made for me. We went to the market but could not find them. After several weeks of searching and asking friends, family, and even the doctor, we discovered the non-fattening potato was really a turnip! It was so easy to stop eating those substitute potatoes!

Big Bubbie lived in the upstairs unit of a duplex. Her son and daughter-in-law lived downstairs. One weekend night, when I was eight, they were all playing cards at the dining room table while I was coloring in a book on the floor. Suddenly there was a flurry of activity. I was able to sneak a look at Big Bubbie, with her eyes closed, on my uncle and aunt's bed. My aunt hustled me upstairs, saying that Big Bubbie was sick. We would wait there for my parents to take me home as soon as possible.

I don't think I ever had an explanation from anyone about how she died. There was a funeral, and she was buried in the cemetery. At least that's what I thought I heard them say. All this was done away from me. They protected me from her death.

Or did they try to protect me from the sights and sounds, leaving me to create my own reality? Today, parents who tune into their children's needs, will be able to understand some of their sorrow and include the children in the rituals that death presents to us. It is called the need for closure.

My childhood was rooted in seriousness, especially after Big Bubbie died. I started working in my parents' store. I guess they couldn't find a babysitter or they wanted me to be with them more often. At such a young age, I was responsible for giving Mom her smelling salts when she felt faint, after smelling food. Big Bubbie and Mom were always extremely close. After Big Bubbie died, the doctor told Mom to work full time in the family store to help grow the business as well as to keep her mind occupied. It was a complex time for my family, but I thought it was normal and logical for the only child, the responsible girl, to help in the family business and help take care of her Mom.

I must have been a teenage infant to be able to grow up so soon! Any resemblance of a carefree, frivolous childhood never returned. I thought I was privileged to be working with my parents, so it never affected me on the conscious level. Those challenges gave me a lifelong attitude of accepting life as very serious. It takes a lot of hard work to overcome adversity,

I called my paternal grandmother Little Bubbie because she was four feet eleven. She had a hard life coming to America after Zadie, my grandfather, had settled in enough at his job to send money for her to travel to America. She did not speak English when she entered through Ellis Island, New York. Zadie died young, leaving her solely responsible for a family of five children. Little Bubbie was a very quiet woman who, without a formal education, did what she had to do to support her family, including taking in laundry and sewing. She taught me, by example, to do what I had to do to survive during very tough times in my life. I just did it!

When television stations started to expand in their numbers and programming, Little Bubbie complained about the horrible wrestling shows on TV. My aunt explained the reality. Wrestling was Little Bubbie's favorite show. Watching and listening from the dining room, we saw her on the edge of the couch yelling and screaming at the bums, telling them to "knock him down, kick him down!"

Remembering my Little Bubbie encourages me to smile inside and grin on the outside! She was an emotionally strong woman who bravely took care of her family, as well as herself, in the best way she knew possible.

Little Bubbie and my mom were very close. They talked on the phone almost daily. When Mom was dying from cancer, Little Bubbie lost patience with not being able to talk with Mom. She became unusually aggressive in demanding that her daughter drive them to our house to see my mom. The stress of hearing about the cancer, in addition to seeing her daughter-in-law so frail and dying, was much too overwhelming. Little Bubbie had a stroke that night. She went into a care facility where she died at age ninety-three. Her lessons of a love and a quiet strength live on within me. I continue to use her positive expressions, such as "It could be worster." When I find myself staying home alone a couple of days in a row, I think about her encouraging me to get out, explore, and "see what the peoples are doing."

I wish I had the opportunity to be close to my two mothers-in-law. How loving and nurturing it could have been to be close like Mom was with Little Bubbie. Unfortunately, they both died before I met either of my husbands. I did have a loving relationship with both of my fathers-in-law.

How very blessed I have been to have the influence of two bubbies. They were unique and balancing influences in my life! My family dropped the descriptions of "little" and "big" when talking about them, but I continue to use my special names for those two special women—my Little Bubbie and my Big Bubbie.

Unfortunately, my son was never able to know my grandmothers. They died before he was born.

**A bubbie is someone with silver in her hair
and gold in her heart!**

19

My Favorite Character

My uncle is a character! Careful now; there are several meanings for the word character. My Uncle Carl is a character of the highest quality. He is my favorite! I've always admired his charm and his appeal in business and social circles. People openly admit they like the way he talks, with a calm maturity. They hear truth coming from a dependable man who is a man of his word.

He can argue one side of an issue and then argue its opposite side, even if he doesn't believe in that point of view. To understand any issue, it is important to be knowledgeable about the subject to the point of truly understanding both sides of it. By being a living example, his lessons empowered me during many discussions.

My uncle was fourteen when I was born. Since he was closer to me in age than any other family member, something prompted me to call him by his first name, rather than Uncle Carl. When he married, the mindset of this logical five year old figured his wife was now an equivalent part of the family, so

I called her by her first name instead of aunt. No one ever questioned me about this, so it never changed. After my son was born, I referred to them as Uncle Carl and Aunt Betty. On several occasions, I asked if this was ever or is now hurtful or uncomfortable for them. Maybe they were being polite by being accepting; I don't know. Recently I started to use their titles of respect whenever I write to them or we talk. It feels right!

I tell the story about how Uncle Carl almost drowned me one day in the swimming pool when I was about seven. We were playing in the water, he with an agenda of teaching me to make friends with water in order to feel safe. He dunked me under the water, and I soon floundered, unable to breathe until he pulled me to the surface. All I could think of while under the water was how I was swallowing enough water that I'd soon die. This traumatic event led to my fear of water and a lifelong dislike of swimming!

Why do I tell you this? I have so many positive feelings along with many stories about my uncle that I don't want you to think he is a made up, perfect person. He is human. Being real takes much more courage than trying to be perfect!

Uncle Carl tells a story about how I, as a toddler, cried while stopped on the steps going up to the second floor of the house. I would not stop crying, so he reached over and pulled my pants down. Shock and awe! Shock and awe! I stopped crying.

Business opportunities required my uncle and aunt to move to Chicago. Mom was a gloomy and lonesome worrywart! Her little brother was so special to our family. My dad was like a big brother to my uncle. Dad gave the family a wake-up call, to convince them my uncle was old enough to cross the street by himself, without holding anyone's hand.

Weekly family dinners allowed us to catch up on events in our lives by sharing stories. When my uncle and aunt moved, we all found excitement in their letters. It wasn't the same.

Mom's family was very business minded. My grandfather had a poultry business during the war. The middle son had a jewelry business. Mom and Dad owned a clothing store, and Uncle Carl took it up a few notches by owning businesses and investing in real estate as an entrepreneur. He is the patriarch of the family, having outlived his siblings by more than forty years. Uncle Carl has continued the pattern of being the loving caretaker of everyone. I admire him for being willing to be an advisor with well thought out ideas. At any age, it's exhausting to continue the role as the strong, willing giver. It's especially challenging for an aging silver sage.

We visited with them a couple of times every year. They returned to Pittsburgh a couple of times each year to visit friends and stayed with us. As much as I looked forward to seeing them, I didn't want them to sleep in our house. The family thought I was a jealous teenager because Mom gave them so much loving attention. Maybe it really was part of my resistance; however, I remember resenting having to give up my room to them in addition to sleeping downstairs on the couch.

The details are more complicated than it seems. The four adults would sit in the kitchen, smoking and talking most of the night. I had to breathe the cigarette smoke in the living room while trying to get to sleep on the couch. They would finally go to bed around four or five in the morning. I gave up my room and breathed the horrible cigarette smoke for what? So they could sit around smoking and talking, which had nothing to do with my sleeping in my own bed, in my airy bedroom! I felt bitterness during their visits. Life goes on, even after breathing all the second hand smoke!

A couple of years ago, my son and I visited with my uncle's family in Chicago. Uncle Carl always enjoyed being the tour guide by finding a variety of places to visit. He would build suspense by telling us about our upcoming adventure, then follow through with fascinating facts and figures about the location.

One day we went to a carnival and walked around, looking at the rides, the games, and the people. When we stopped in front of the ferris wheel to discuss which direction would be next, my son wanted to go on the ride. I agreed to buy him a ticket, but he would have to go alone because the ferris wheel was too daunting for me. My uncle immediately insisted upon going on the ride with his great nephew.

Aunt Betty told me Uncle Carl had stopped going on rides many years ago. She strongly encouraged me to take his place before it was too late. I couldn't, I wouldn't go on the ferris wheel, not even for my son. After everyone argued, my uncle took Hal by the arm, gently insisting they go on the ride together! They made it through the entire ride, which resulted in my son happily smiling and thinking it was terrific. Meanwhile, I think my uncle was about to throw up. We just kept on walking to other areas of the carnival to continue sightseeing. What he did for love!

I always had a secure feeling that if I was ever in real trouble, ever in real need, I could go to my uncle. One time, I remember being in a panic because my husband and I were in a terrible financial bind. I was trying to figure out how we could live in the park since there weren't any more paths to take to solve our financial problems!

As last resort, I asked Uncle Carl for help with money. I was not at all confident he would help us, but, to my delight, he came through. Yes, he saved us from being homeless during agonizing financial times. I learned how love is in the heart, the soul, and the mind. It is not just buying gifts or attending special family functions and then going out of sight and out of mind. My Uncle Carl is in my heart all the time. He is my hero!

Even though the family continues to live in Chicago and I have lived in Los Angeles for over forty years, we have always felt close to each other. I don't really understand why we never saw each other more often. Life does go on with its financial problems, job stresses, health problems, and many joys to share. Perhaps our feelings were so strong we did not feel the need to renew them by scheduled visits. We did take advantage of how easy it was not to work at crossing the country by airplane for visits. What if I could rewrite the scripts of our lives? What if... What if...

Our bond comes from feeling the love. We know permanent caring is not just a bandage to cover wounds.

20

The Gift of Life

Have you ever noticed how much easier things seem in memory than they were when we actually experienced them?

Childbirth is an excellent example. Doctoring, testing, scheduling, and record keeping consumed my life, when I wasn't in the classroom teaching other people's children. Then the magical day came when the doctor smiled and nodded his head yes. I screamed "Yes? I'm pregnant? There's a baby in there?" It was a high-risk pregnancy because of my advanced child bearing age of thirty eight. Lots of boring bed rest was the order for the duration of the pregnancy. No complaints, we were having a baby, a miracle, a dream come true, the gift of life!

It was September, the beginning of a new school year. I could not imagine school starting without me in the classroom. For the previous seventeen years, teaching had been my life. A substitute teacher took over until the doctor cleared me to return to work. School not only started without me, but the school year finished without me too! Tuning into the needs of my little gift of life, I followed doctor's orders to stay as stress free and movement free as possible.

I felt nauseous and sick only once, when I ate a big breakfast of eggs instead of my usual non-nourishing toast. Eating only what was good for that growing fetus became an obsession. Feeling queasy for the first three months and again for the last three months, in addition to not being able to leave the house, well...those are parts of the story I don't care about enough to remember the details.

So many pregnant women hate the combination of weight gain plus looking fat, but I was proud of them. I wanted to show off my expanding belly to everyone! Wearing the same maternity clothes over and over was not at all interesting, but I didn't care about not having a variety of clothes, because being home bound took over for being fashionable. I was having a miracle baby! I was finally going to fit into the women's society known as being a mommy!

We attended Lamaze classes and learned about cesarean sections to be prepared either way. The YMCA classes were very helpful for us to learn to feed a baby by nursing or by bottle, and how to diaper a baby doll. While diapering the baby doll, the soon to be dad kept dropping it off the table. The class had a good laugh over it and predicted that we were going to have a slippery baby! There is so much to learn about having a real, innocent, helpless little baby. I read every self-help book I could buy or borrow from the library. Those were the days before computers. Now it's easy to access information while staying at home.

Oh my, I kept feeling I had to go to the bathroom. After two days of the pressure getting worse and more frequent, I called the doctor. He told me repeatedly to avoid Thursdays, his day off. "Deliver any day or time of the week, except a Thursday." I called him Wednesday night, apologized, then asked if I should go to the hospital. He told me to take my time, go easy, but go now.

Our recent tour of the hospital included a warning to make sure not to arrive at the hospital close to 11:00 p.m. Hang in there and wait because the insurance will charge you an extra day if you get there before 11:00 p.m. Yes, we arrived at 10:20 p.m. The insurance considered those forty minutes another whole day.

So far, this direction follower was not following doctor's rules or insurance regulations, but I was too nervous and excited to care about them. When the bewildering, uncomfortable physical feelings would take over, the fear of the unknown kept me doing whatever needed to be done.

Our baby, a happy and healthy boy, was born by natural childbirth at 10:24 Thursday morning. When I looked at my beautiful little baby boy, I really did forget about all the trauma and drama of the pregnancy. It didn't matter anymore, and it still doesn't matter anymore. I had my baby boy, Hal Edward, my gift of life.

Yes, we wanted another baby. First a boy, then a girl, was always our plan. I'm so grateful the first half of my dream came true. A very long time was required for me to cope with knowing, and then accepting the reality. I did not get pregnant again. It just didn't happen. Some things are not meant to be. Hal is an only child, just like his mom and dad.

As a former teacher and perfectionist, I wanted to do all the right things for my baby. Most baby talk words sounded silly to me. Foods have names that do not sound like "num-nums." Bottles are not "botties." It isn't logical for me to go into a store and ask to purchase a large "num-num" or "bottie," so why teach made up baby talk to babies?

My seriousness even overwhelmed me! When I spoke at a higher pitch than usual and repeated words in a singsong fashion, like adults do when talking to children, the sounds were real English words. I wanted my baby to have the advantages of everything I could learn to do so he would be a healthy, well-adjusted child. Speaking clearly and reading with emphasis came naturally to this teacher/mom. I was his main caretaker, so it was up to me to nurture my gift of life in the best way possible. I did it all! Super Mom! Parenting is a skill set unlike any other. I'm grateful for the opportunities presented along with the patience and energy to deal with the challenges.

Responsibilities for giving life never end. The dentist's nurse said she was twenty eight and wanted a baby this year. The dentist was joking when he told me he would retire in seven years and then she can have babies. I asked if she was prepared to be a loving mom for the rest of her life.

The gift of life is a huge lifetime of responsibility. The nurse responded by saying it was fine; she would take care of her child until he or she moved out at eighteen, and then the youngster would be a self-sufficient adult.

After a quiet chuckle, then a controlled laugh, I told her that my son, twenty-nine at the time, was part of the boomerang generation. He moved out then moved back in with me a couple of times. Her immediate reaction was to say she wouldn't allow such a boomerang to happen. Her family would prepare for any grown child to leave home, just as she did. Then she ran out of the room crying and sobbing about no one wanting her to have a baby. Reality is tough!

She didn't ask for a roadmap to childrearing. The dentist and I overstepped our boundaries by trying to share the challenges with her. Learning never ends. Seniors want to share their valuable understandings, life experiences, and wisdom. Sometimes we have to listen and resist being resourceful.

So many unexpected questions and problems come with being a new parent. We think things will magically be fine, even though we don't automatically receive any training for taking care of a child.

For example, there were questions and decisions about the handling of money during many stages of my son's life. Parents frequently can't find common ground with each other on money issues, so how are they supposed to know how to pass down responsible money values to their children? It must be done! My son and I never agreed on money matters. He is a spender while I'm a saver. I believe as long as I take conscientious care of my money, it will take care of me. I'm doing my best to step aside and observe how he is developing skills to do it his own way. I have to constantly remind myself to accept that he has to lead his life, his way. Being a Mom does not have a shut off valve, it's a lifetime commitment.

Parents decide their family involvement in religion. If they follow the same religion, then the road is certainly easier. If not, there is a lot to figure out on a constant basis regarding values, morals, and beliefs. I've changed my view on religion many, many times. My son has accepted our family religion but knows he is free to tweak it to suit his lifestyle, and he does just that, to modernize his religious beliefs.

My parents gave me the gift of life, like we gave the same gift to our son. One step at a time, one day at a time. As an only child, I had little experience with babies, those limited to the years when I worked as a babysitter. When I was age twelve, I was left alone with a three month old infant for five hours. I was a kid, what did I know about babies? Why would new parents trust a preteen? Mom assured me she would be near the phone all evening in case I needed help. I think I called her about eight times. Even then, I was trying to be a super preteen!

I know it's true. I take my familial responsibilities very seriously. We are talking about being responsible for another life. What could be more serious? If we didn't enjoy the laughter, successes, and love that families share, life would be full of conflict! Lately, my miracle son has shown his response to my being serious, worried, and motherly by saying, "That's my Mom, being Mom!"

**There are two ways to lead life:
One is as though nothing is a miracle.
The other is as though everything is a miracle.**

21

Designing a New Life

Sometimes, leaving the birth city of your discomfort to venture into the wilderness of your intuition becomes necessary. What you can discover will be wonderful. What you will discover is yourself!

Living in Pittsburgh was becoming a continuing source of unhappiness for me. As more evidence was pointing to my life becoming stagnant, I felt increasing stress coupled with hopelessness. My attention was focused on teaching by day and taking care of family by night but not on having my own life. I questioned how, when, and if my turn would come to live my dream life. How could I design a new life without finding opportunities to discover new friends and activities?

Mom was in the magical five year waiting period to find out if her cancer had spread. I was looking at life if she healed, as well as life if her health became worse. What was the future holding for me? The popular expression of the time was "Today is the first day of the rest of your life." There was the answer, telling me life would remain the same, life would continue as usual. If, and realistically when, my mom died, how was I going to function without her? Dad would be alone as he aged and would need me.

A friend pointed out several times, in a joking manner, how I had missed opportunities because I was at the airport when my ship came in! I felt such a deep responsibility to be there for my parents that I could not find a separate life for myself. Never once did I reflect on the fact they had each other, friends, and family.

The socioeconomic environment was changing in Pittsburgh. Industries were retooling and revamping their operations. People my age were moving away to find better careers. One year I joined every singles social group available for a twenty three year old. The grand total amounted to one. What's more, I was the youngest person in the group. Most members were age forty or older. In the span of a year, I had one blind date, followed by a year without going out at all. I felt a growing resentment building inside of me, against everyone and everything.

Surely, options were available for me to have a life of my own. I needed to press the reset button, which I knew meant eventually moving out of Pittsburgh. Instead of thinking of this as running away from my problems, I viewed it as running toward a new life, also known as getting a life! I was afraid of someday regretting not leaving now. I would become too old or too imbedded in this Pittsburgh life, making getting away impossible. It takes self-confidence, especially for an only child, to move 3,000 miles away from family to start a new life. I had only one friend, so friendships were not a big pressure in this mix. How was I going to find the confidence to move? The only solution was to ignite a spark to enable me to see things in a new light. Showing up for life isn't enough.

When I visited with cousins in Los Angeles, and attended a UCLA scholarship summer program for teachers, I felt comfortable there. Just to make comparisons between the Los Angeles Schools and the Pittsburgh Schools, I interviewed with the local school district. Then I returned to my life in Pittsburgh. A few months later, I received a letter offering me a teaching position in Los Angeles. My parents and I talked about it while laughing. I joked, wondering if they expected me to commute across country!

Next came a winter with the coldest weather ever. Temperatures went down to twenty degrees below zero. The roads were icy, making transportation everywhere scary and dangerous. While I was driving, the car tires skidded, prompting me to yell out, "Why do I exist in this miserable weather when I could live in nice, comfortable, warm Los Angeles?" Of course, no one answered my questions. Not this time!

I had a serious discussion with my parents about moving to what I perceived as a better life. Dad would not discuss it at all. He believed the current consensus of the time, which dictated that a young woman live at home until she got married. Nice girls did not move out of their parents' home! Mom acted bravely, asking questions because she knew I deserved more than what was available to me at the time, in Pittsburgh.

More research had to be done and many more questions had to be asked and answered before anything real could be decided. I did have an offer to teach in Los Angeles, sitting on my desk at home.

A teacher in the school where I taught in the primary grades, said she wanted to visit her brother in Los Angeles the next summer. We talked about my teaching job offer and the ramifications of my "running away from home." Irene suggested we drive across country together so I'd have my car there. During the vacation in Los Angeles, she could drive her brother's car. Then she could travel back home by airplane, making everything manageable for both of us. Problem solved? Not quite.

My cousins in Los Angeles offered for me to stay with them until I was assigned to a school, which would make finding an apartment easier. Things fell into place at such a natural tempo. Amazing how I was swept into the tide of change. The emotional tensions at home were quite thick with mixed feelings. We all wanted me to be happy, but why so far from home?

Mom always loved my red Chevy convertible. I bought a new car for my new life, and gave the red car to Mom. It was only three years old, in great condition, and paid off. Mom was ecstatic to have her own car! I have a photo of Mom standing next to the car, pointing at it and asking, "Mine?" It is a wonderful picture showing her pride and excitement. Everyone felt more comfortable knowing I was driving a new car to my new life across the country. Those sharing, caring arrangements worked out ideally for everyone.

Right after the school year ended, one June morning at five o'clock, I anxiously peeled away from the curb in my new car and started toward my new life. The mechanic had inspected the car thoroughly. I had loaded it down with personal items and checked everything at least twice. I was on my way to a great new adventure, starting with driving to my traveling friend's house.

When I arrived, Irene nervously pushed me into her kitchen to call my dad immediately. With tears in my eyes and panic in my stomach, I called him. Dad said the left taillight on the car was burned out. He wanted to make sure I was aware to stop to get the bulb replaced. Then he ended the conversation with, "Be careful, Baby. I love you."

Irene and I drove on and on, during very long days to rush to California in five days. I had to be available to meet with the employment division of the Los Angeles Schools. Mom and Dad put a map of the United States on the kitchen wall, next to the phone. They were easily able to follow my progress across the states. Every night I called home to check in, so they knew our current location. During those brief conversations, Mom stifled her emotions. She bravely struggled with trying to sound brave and encouraging.

I hurried up, rushed to get to Los Angeles for the school placement meeting, only to sit and wait. In August, they assigned me to a school in a nice area, where I eventually rented a nearby apartment.

Mom died three years later. Dad died thirty seven years later. No one has an accurate crystal ball showing what might have happened if I had not designed a new life for myself. Things unfolded as they were meant to be.

Pittsburgh, Pa. is now known as the best place for seniors to live. Miami, Fl. comes in second. Pittsburgh has wonderful medical, transportation, and living facilities, as well as other services for seniors.

So here I am, full circle as a senior, back at the beginning with struggles to design a new life. People have always asked me if I would move back East. Family members still urge me to return. Several of my cousins and their families live there.

My decision to design a new life has never changed. I like living in the Los Angeles area with its ideal weather, friendly people, and vast variety of things to do. I've never had any desire to live any other place.

Many seniors talk about living their retirement years where housing, food, and daily goods are less expensive. I definitely understand and completely agree with their motivation. When it comes to discovering my new life as a silver sage, I know as long as I can afford it, I want to live in my current comfort zone.

I will be true to myself, design a new life as a retiree, while continuing on my life journey. Today is the first day of the rest of my new life as a silver sage!

Success comes in cans: failure in can nots.

Conclusion

At the beginning of this book writing process, I wanted the reader to feel motivated to improve life by finding an open door to develop a new mind set for innovative experiences.

I hope I succeeded in inspiring you to write your life story or personal resume. Get started, see how it goes. Start with thinking, then wondering, and then smiling. Take your time, let it happen. No pressure, no time constraints. If it does not happen today, try again tomorrow. Learn from everyone, everywhere.

This journey of writing led me to open the window to my soul. While exploring the depths of past events, I was able to understand how the many people, places, and events have made me the person I am today. This awareness gave me the confidence to let go of old thinking, old decisions, plus old stuff!

Writing opened up a sense of humor hiding somewhere in me. It's okay to be silly! It takes the pressure off the seriousness of daily life. Writing guided me to recognize how the past is the past. It's over, it's done. I met many people during this journey. Recently, I even found myself!

**You are one of a kind.
Like unique finger prints
Be the best that you can be!**

So here we are together, at the end of this book adventure. Endings are beginnings! I wonder where you and I will go with this new start. I'll see you there!

LaVergne, TN USA
05 December 2010
207449LV00001B/159/P